PLASTIC CANVAS
Seasonal Sensations

PLASTIC CANVAS
Seasonal Sensations

Decorating your home for each special season has never been more fun! And creating clever gifts for loved ones has never been easier. With this collection of plastic canvas needlepoint designs at your fingertips, you'll have everything you need to make every season of the year a sensational celebration.

Welcome springtime with a bevy of bunnies, chicks and other fun critters made into baskets and fashion accessories. You'll be ready for the new baby in your family with beautiful pastel baby accessories, and Mother's Day will be brighter than ever with a gorgeous ribbons-and-lace dresser set.

Summer celebrations will be festive with watermelons, ladybugs and Uncle Sam designs. Create a special wall hanging or valet box to present to Dad on Father's Day.

For fall, decorate an entryway or buffet with a whimsical scarecrow complete with pumpkins and raffia straw stuffing. A detailed pumpkin caddy will hold your oven-fresh cookies, while angels and choral singers will help you get the jump on holiday preparations.

Winter brings time for leisurely games of chess by the fire and time for stitching gifts that say "I love you" for family and friends. Cheery snowmen adorn a frosty garland and decorations, and a beautiful, ornate dish will hold your favorite winter potpourri.

If plastic canvas needlepoint is new to you, take a peek at Ready, Set, Stitch on page 154. You'll find everything you need to know about stitches, yarns, canvas and much, much more.

Happy Stitching!

PUBLISHER / Donna Robertson
EDITORIAL DIRECTOR / Carolyn Brooks Christmas
DESIGN DIRECTOR / Fran Rohus
CREATIVE DIRECTOR / Greg Smith
PRODUCTION DIRECTOR / Ange Workman

EDITORIAL
EDITOR / Janet Tipton
COORDINATING EDITOR / Jennifer A. Simcik
ASSOCIATE EDITORS / Kristine Hart, Margie Kiepke
EDITORIAL ASSISTANTS / Janice Kellenberger, Jessica Rice
PUBLISHER'S ASSISTANT / Marianne Telesca
PROOFREADER / Mary Lingle

ART
ART DIRECTOR / Greg Smith
ASSISTING ART DIRECTORS / Rusty Lingle, Minette Collins Smith
PHOTOGRAPHERS / Renée Agee, Tammy Cromer-Campbell, Mary Craft
PHOTO STYLIST / Teresa S. Hannaway
COVER PHOTO / Tammy Cromer-Campbell, Joe Lingle

PRODUCTION
ASSISTANT PRODUCTION DIRECTOR / Betty Gibbs-Radla
PRODUCTION MANAGER / Karen White
PRODUCTION / Glenda Chamberlain, Derek Gentry, Diane Simpson
TECHNICAL DIRECTOR/PRODUCTION / John J. Nosal

DESIGN
DESIGN COORDINATOR / Brenda Wendling

BUSINESS
PRESIDENT / Jerry Gentry
VICE PRESIDENT/CUSTOMER SERVICE / Karen Pierce
VICE PRESIDENT/MARKETING / Greg Deily
VICE PRESIDENT/M.I.S. / John Trotter

CREDITS

Sincerest thanks to all the designers, manufacturers and other
professionals whose dedication has made this book possible.
Special thanks to Klaus Rothe of Sullivan Rothe Design, Berne, IN,
Tom Buckley of JTM Colorscan, Ft. Worth, TX, and
Katie Dunbar of Semline Printing, Boston, MA.

Library of Congress Cataloging in Publication Data
ISBN: 0-9638031-0-7
First Printing: 1993
Library of Congress Catalog Card Number: 93-85500
Published and Distributed by *The Needlecraft Shop, Inc.*
Printed in the United States of America.

Dear Friend,

It's here at last — a big, beautiful collection of brand-new, exciting plastic canvas designs in one colorful keepsake volume. Within these pages, you'll find over 80 delightful projects, each complete with easy-to-follow instructions in large type, color graphs and diagrams, and a dazzling, full-color photograph.

The designers have really knocked themselves out, creating smashing original designs to help you express your decorating and gift-giving talents in each season of the year. Each project is fun to make and is sure to get lots of oohs and aahs from family and friends after it's completed.

Whether you are a beginning stitcher or seasoned needlecrafter, you'll find everything you need to begin here. A celebration of the fun and versatility of plastic canvas needlepoint, this collection is designed to inspire you to create clever creations to enhance the beauty and enjoyment of each season. This book has been a joy to produce, and on behalf of everyone here at The Needlecraft Shop, I wish you the very best in your stitching endeavors.

Warmest Regards,

Carolyn

Carolyn Christmas

CONTENTS

74

Spring

Bears, bunnies and ducks decorate baskets and baby accessories, and a beautiful, ribbon-trimmed dresser set will be the perfect gift for Mom. These gifts are as fresh as a May morning!

Summer

Luscious watermelons make summer entertaining light and easy. Dad is sure to love a gift stitched especially for him, and everyone will love this colorful selection of fun warm-weather ideas.

13

Autumn

A friendly scarecrow will stand guard over all your autumn goodies while you get a head start on holiday decorating ideas with heavenly angel designs.

Winter

Your winter will sparkle and shine with cheerful snowmen, ice skates and pretty bows. Create gifts that say "I love you" with hearts and flowers on greeting cards, kitchen accessories and more.

A Breath of Spring

As cool March winds dissolve into April showers and warm May sunshine, a feeling of celebration fills the air! It's a time for sharing pretty gifts on Mother's Day, welcoming the new baby with whimsical accessories, or brightening your home with fresh colors and breezy touches. 🐦

Photographed at *Glory Bee Honeycomb Suites*, Gladewater, Texas.

SENSATIONS

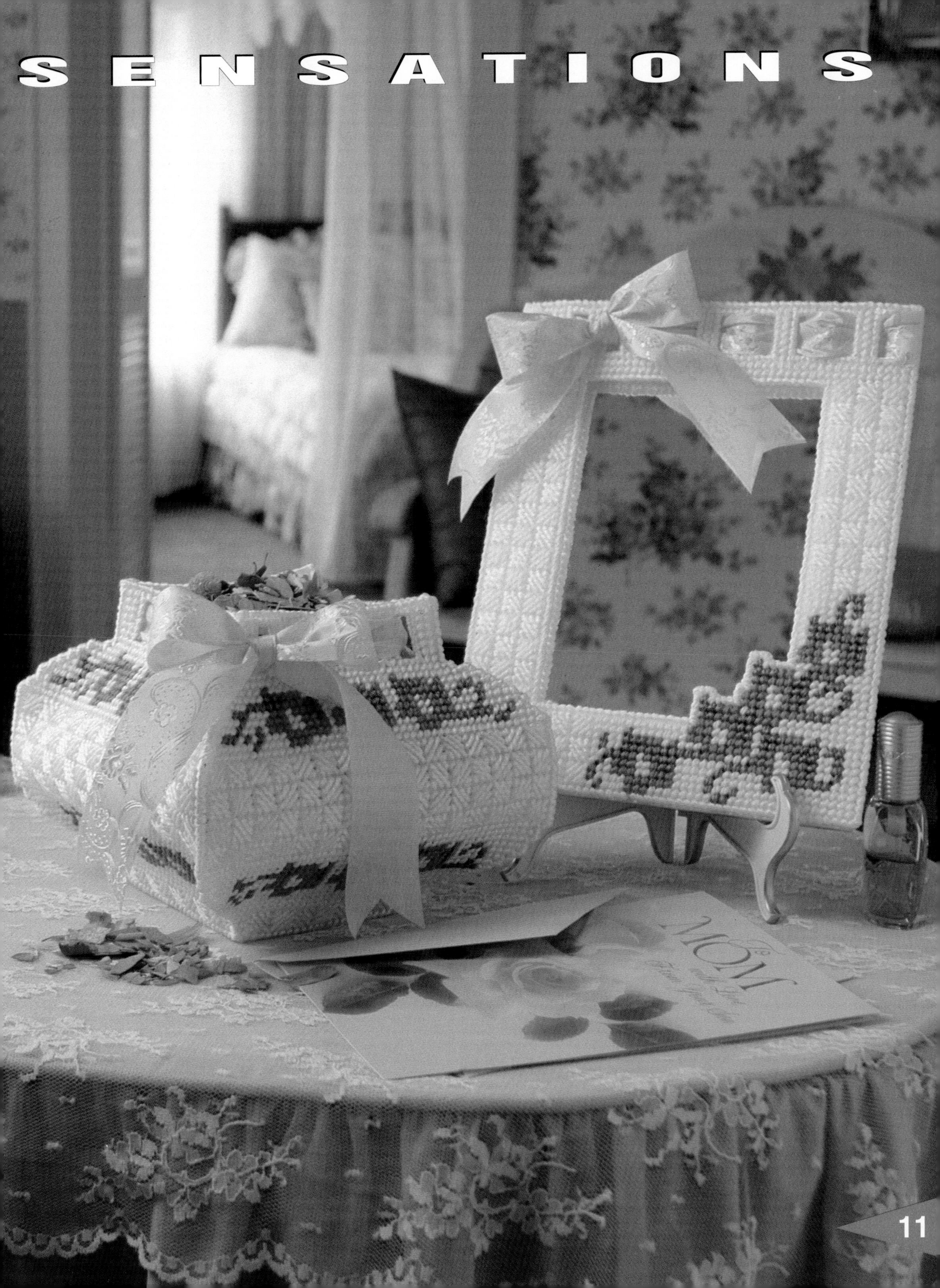

Welcome the new baby with an adorable baby animal basket filled with a selection of small gifts. Later, the basket will decoratively serve as a changing table catch-all to keep the nursery tidy. Older children will delight in receiving one of these spring baskets filled with special treats.

BENJAMIN BEAR

BEATRICE BUNNY

Li'l Critters
GIFT BASKETS

BY CAROLYN CHRISTMAS

DAPHNE DUCK BASKET

SIZE: 6⅛" across x 9¾" tall.
SKILL LEVEL: Average
MATERIALS: 1½ sheets of 7-count plastic canvas; One 6" plastic canvas radial circle; Two 20-mm. wiggle eyes; Craft glue or glue gun; Worsted-weight or plastic canvas yarn (for amounts see Color Key on page 14).

CUTTING INSTRUCTIONS:
(See graphs on pages 14 and 15.)
A: For side pieces, cut two 20 x 68 holes.
B: For bottom, use canvas circle.
C: For handle pieces, cut two 4 x 64 holes.
D: For body, cut one according to graph.
E: For wings, cut two according to graph.
F: For feet, cut two according to graph.
G: For bill, cut two according to graph.

STITCHING INSTRUCTIONS:
1: For basket, overlapping at each short end and working through both thicknesses to join as indicated on graphs, using colors and stitches indicated, work A pieces according to Side 1 and Side 2 graphs. With Sail Blue and easing to fit, Whipstitch side and unworked B together, forming basket.
2: Overlapping five holes at one end of each piece and working

DAPHNE DUCK

through both thicknesses to join, using Sail Blue and Slanted Gobelin Stitch over narrow width, work C pieces; Overcast unfinished long edges of handle. Overcast unfinished top edge of basket, catching one short end of handle over each side seam as you work to join.

3: Using colors and stitches indicated, work D, E (one on opposite side of canvas), F and G pieces according to graphs. With matching colors, Overcast unfinished edges of D, E and F pieces. Holding G pieces wrong sides together, with Bright Orange, Whipstitch together as indicated; Overcast unfinished edges.

NOTE: Cut one 6" length of Baby Yellow.

4: For hair, thread 6" strand of Baby Yellow through top edge of head at center; tie in square knot. Trim to about 1½"; fray ends. Matching bottom edges, glue feet and body to basket, and wings, bill and eyes to duck as shown in photo. Glue tip of each wing to handle as shown.❀

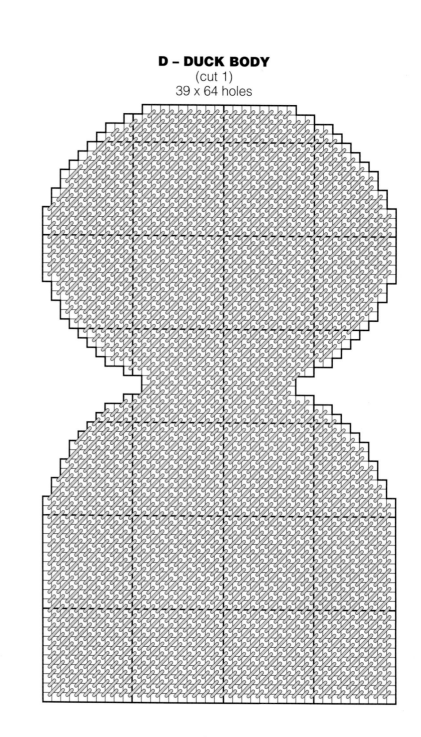

For Baby's Safety

As the baby begins to toddle, he'll enjoy carrying his toys in these baskets. A smiling baby animal basket can make picking up and putting away toys fun for even the smallest child! If you intend to let the child play with the basket, there are a few extra precautions you can take to be sure the basket is safe.

Instead of using glue-on wiggle eyes, use sew-on eyes. When assembling the baskets, use a hot glue gun, and for extra security, sew components together with clear fishing line. Sewing on eyes with clear fishing line or quilting thread will make the stitches more secure than regular thread. To make the bunny's pom-pom nose more secure, leave two yarn ends 6" long when trimming pom-pom. Thread these ends through to back of head; tie securely in knot and weave in about 3" of tails. Clip. Place a dot of hot glue over knot at back of head.

D – DUCK BODY
(cut 1)
39 x 64 holes

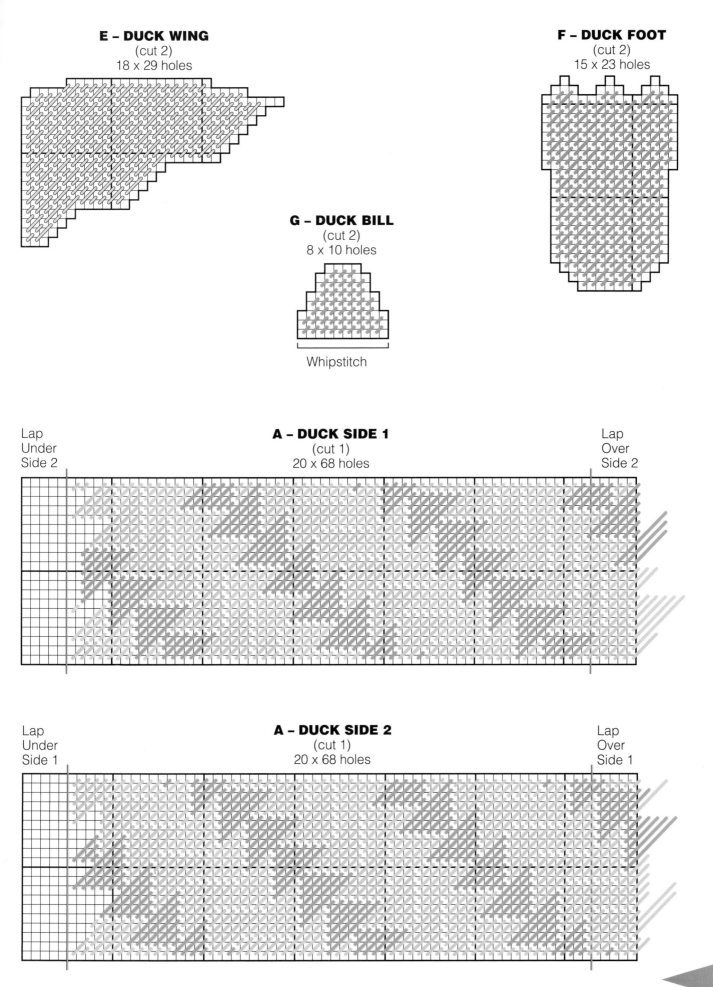

E – DUCK WING
(cut 2)
18 x 29 holes

F – DUCK FOOT
(cut 2)
15 x 23 holes

G – DUCK BILL
(cut 2)
8 x 10 holes

Whipstitch

A – DUCK SIDE 1
(cut 1)
20 x 68 holes

Lap
Under
Side 2

Lap
Over
Side 2

A – DUCK SIDE 2
(cut 1)
20 x 68 holes

Lap
Under
Side 1

Lap
Over
Side 1

15

BEATRICE BUNNY BASKET

SIZE: About 7⅛" across x about 12½" tall.

SKILL LEVEL: Average

MATERIALS: Two sheets of 7-count plastic canvas; One 9½" plastic canvas radial circle; Two 20-mm. wiggle eyes; 1½" cardboard; Craft glue or glue gun; Worsted-weight or plastic canvas yarn (for amounts see Color Key).

CUTTING INSTRUCTIONS:

A: For side pieces, cut one 21 x 77 holes and one 21 x 76 holes.

B: For bottom, cut outer 8 rows of holes off canvas circle to measure 7" across.

C: For handle pieces, cut two 4 x 64 holes.

BUNNY BASKET STITCH PATTERN GUIDE

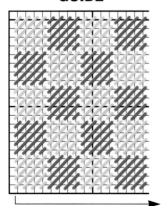

Continue established pattern across each entire piece.

D: For body, cut one according to Daphne Duck D Graph on page 14.

E: For arms, cut two according to graph.

F: For feet, cut two according to graph.

G: For ears, cut two according to graph.

H: For muzzle pieces, cut two according to graph.

STITCHING INSTRUCTIONS:

1: For basket, overlapping five holes at one end and four holes at opposite end and working through both thicknesses to join at overlap areas, using colors and stitches indicated, work A pieces according to Bunny Basket Stitch Pattern Guide. With Lilac, Whipstitch side and unworked B together, forming basket.

2: Substituting Lilac for Sail Blue, follow Step 2 of Daphne Duck Basket on page 13.

3: Using Baby Blue for body and colors and stitches indicated, work D-H pieces according to graphs; with matching colors, Overcast unfinished edges.

NOTE: For pom-pom nose, wrap Baby Pink around 1½" cardboard 40 times. Slide loops off card-board, and tie a separate length of yarn tightly around center of all loops. Cut loops and trim to 1".

4: Glue feet and body to basket, and arms, ears, muzzle pieces, nose and eyes to bunny as shown in photo. Glue each arm to handle as shown. ✿

E – BUNNY ARM
(cut 2)
11 x 28 holes

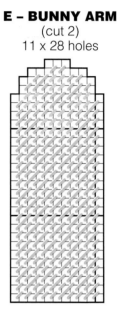

F – BUNNY FOOT
(cut 2)
16 x 27 holes

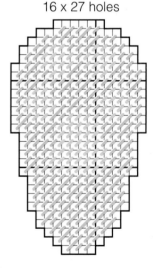

G – BUNNY EAR
(cut 2)
9 x 32 holes

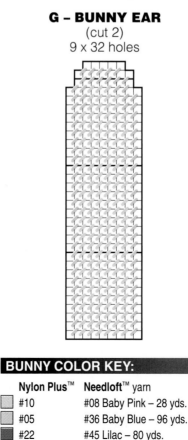

H – BUNNY MUZZLE PIECE
(cut 2)
14 x 14 holes

BUNNY COLOR KEY:

Nylon Plus™	Needloft™ yarn
#10	#08 Baby Pink – 28 yds.
#05	#36 Baby Blue – 96 yds.
#22	#45 Lilac – 80 yds.

BENJAMIN BEAR BASKET

SIZE: 7⅛" across x 9¾" tall.
SKILL LEVEL: Average
MATERIALS: Two sheets of 7-count plastic canvas; One 9½" plastic canvas radial circle; Two 20-mm. wiggle eyes; Craft glue or glue gun; Worsted-weight or plastic canvas yarn (for amounts see Color Key).

CUTTING INSTRUCTIONS:

A: For side pieces, cut two 19 x 75 holes.

B: For bottom, cut outer 8 rows of holes off canvas circle to measure 7" across.

C: For handle pieces, cut two 4 x 64 holes.

D: For body, cut one according to Daphne Duck D Graph on page 14.

E: For arms, cut two according to Beatrice Bunny E Graph.

F: For feet, cut two according to graph.

G: For ears, cut two according to graph.

H: For muzzle, cut one according to graph.

I: For nose, cut one according to graph.

STITCHING INSTRUCTIONS:

1: For basket, overlapping three holes at one end and two holes at opposite end and working through both thicknesses to join at overlap areas, using colors and stitches indicated, work A pieces according to Bear Basket Stitch Pattern Guide. With Sail Blue and easing to fit, Whipstitch side and unworked B together, forming basket.

2: Follow Step 2 of Daphne Duck Basket on page 13.

3: Using Maple for body and colors and stitches indicated, and substituting Beige for Baby Blue on arms, work D-I pieces according to graphs. With Beige for arms, Maple for feet and ears and with matching colors, Overcast unfinished edges of D-I pieces. Using Black and Straight Stitch, embroider mouth as indicated on H graph.

4: Glue feet and body to basket, and arms, ears, muzzle, nose and eyes to bear as shown in photo. Glue each arm to handle as shown. ✿

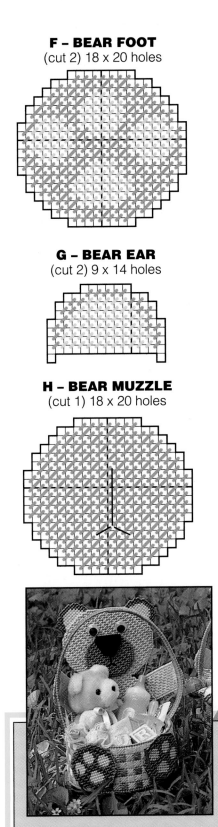

F – BEAR FOOT
(cut 2) 18 x 20 holes

G – BEAR EAR
(cut 2) 9 x 14 holes

H – BEAR MUZZLE
(cut 1) 18 x 20 holes

BEAR BASKET STITCH PATTERN GUIDE

Continue established pattern across each entire piece.

I – BEAR NOSE
(cut 1)
8 x 10 holes

BEAR COLOR KEY:

	Nylon Plus™	Needloft™ yarn
■	#02	#00 Black – 3 yds.
▨	#10	#08 Baby Pink – 10 yds.
▨	#35	#13 Maple – 22 yds.
▨	#04	#35 Sail Blue – 40 yds.
▨	#05	#36 Baby Blue – 20 yds.
□	#43	#40 Beige – 68 yds.
▨	#01	#41 White – 20 yds.

Gift Basket Ideas

Baskets of goodies make such wonderful gifts, because they can be filled with the perfect selection of gifts chosen especially for the recipient. They're fun to fill and need not be expensive. These darling baby animal gift baskets can be filled imaginatively to please not only the new baby, but Mom as well.

A waiting Mom-to-be will love a basket filled with goodies just for her. She'll use the basket later in the baby's room — but for now, she'll love getting things chosen just for her in the midst of all the baby gifts. Fill the basket with bubble bath, a paperback novel by her favorite author and some healthy edibles that you know she'll like.

SIZE: Worked piece is 4⅞" x 12".

SKILL LEVEL: Easy

MATERIALS: ½ sheet of 7-count plastic canvas; Frame or mat and frame with 4½" x 11½" opening; #3 pearl cotton or six-strand embroidery floss (for amount see Color Key); Worsted-weight or plastic canvas yarn (for amounts see Color Key).

CUTTING INSTRUCTIONS:

A: For Splish Splash, cut one 33 x 80 holes.

STITCHING INSTRUCTIONS:

1: Using yarn colors indicated and Continental Stitch, work A according to graph. Fill in uncoded areas using Baby Blue and Continental Stitch. Using pearl cotton or six strands floss, French Knot, Straight Stitch and Lazy Daisy Stitch, embroider eyes, antennae and wing detail as indicated on graph.

2: Do not Overcast unfinished edges. Frame as desired.❈

A – SPLISH SPLASH
(cut 1)
33 x 80 holes

COLOR KEY:

#3 pearl cotton or floss

■ Black – 1 yd.

Nylon Plus™	Needloft™ yarn
■ #02	#00 Black – small amount
#50	#12 Pumpkin – 3 yds.
▨ #41	#19 Straw – 9 yds.
▨ #48	#25 Moss – 2 yds.
■ #31	#27 Holly – 10 yds.
□ #05	#36 Baby Blue – 16 yds.
#17	#58 Bright Orange – 1 yd.
#55	#59 Plum – 2 yds.

STITCH KEY:

— Backstitch/Straight Stitch

● French Knot

⌒ Lazy Daisy Stitch

SPLISH SPLASH

BY MICHELE WILCOX

Brighten up your bath with this trio of playful yellow ducks. They're out for a stroll in the warm spring sunshine with the hope of finding an irresistible puddle!

PASTEL KEEPSAKES

BY KATHRYN BATH SCHALLER

Trim these tiny, quick-to-stitch treasures with delicate pearls, lace and silk flowers. They're delightful as package trims, bridal shower favors or table decorations.

C: For Hat top pieces, cut three according to graph.

D: For Open Basket and Standing Basket top, cut one each according to graph.

E: For Standing Basket base, cut one according to graph.

F: For Fold-over Basket, cut one according to graph.

STITCHING INSTRUCTIONS:

1: Using white and stitches indicated, work A, one B (leaving uncoded area unworked), one C, D (overlap ends and work through both thicknesses to join as indicated on graph), E (overlap one hole at ends and work through both thicknesses to join as indicated) and F pieces according to graphs. Overcast unfinished edges of D-F pieces.

2: For Hat center, holding unworked B pieces together on wrong side of worked piece and working through all thicknesses, Whipstitch together. For Hat top, Whipstitch C pieces together as for Hat center. Glue Hat center to center of brim, and top to Hat center at unworked area. Glue lace around top edge of brim, prestrung pearls over lace and to inner edge of Hat center as shown in photo. Tie about 12" of narrow ribbon into a bow around base of hat center; glue to secure and trim

SIZE: Hat is 3¾" across; Open Basket is 1⅝" x 3½"; Standing Basket is 2¼" x 3⅜" x 2½" tall; Fold-over Basket is 4" long.

SKILL LEVEL: Average

MATERIALS FOR ONE OF EACH: (NOTE: Choose notions and floral items in desired pastel colors or white.) One sheet of 10-count plastic canvas; 1 yd. of ¾" pregathered lace; 1½ yds. of ⅛"-½" satin ribbon; 1¼ yds. of prestrung 2-mm. pearls; 24" of 3-mm. pearl spray; Small silk or paper forget-me-nots (at least 42); One ⅜" ribbon rose cluster; Craft glue or glue gun; #5 pearl cotton or six-strand embroidery floss (for amount see Color Key on page 22).

CUTTING INSTRUCTIONS:
(See graphs on page 22.)

A: For Hat brim, cut one according to graph.

B: For Hat center pieces, cut six according to graph.

ends. Glue several flowers to Hat opposite bow as shown.

3: For Open Basket, glue lace around bottom edge of basket, flowers around top edge and wide ribbon across length of handle as shown.

4: For Standing Basket, with tall edges of base at curved side edges of basket, glue remaining D and E pieces together. Glue lace around bottom edge of basket and narrow ribbon to underside of lace and around bottom edge of base as shown. Glue flowers around top edge of basket and ribbon across

length of handle as shown. Tie ribbon into two small bows; trim ends. Glue one flower and one bow to each end of handle as shown.

NOTES: Cut pearl spray into 4" lengths. Separate ribbon roses.

5: For Fold-over Basket, folding F wrong sides together, glue handle edges together. Glue six rose stems and three lengths of pearl spray to inside of basket at each end. Avoiding handles, glue lace around bottom edge of basket. Glue three rows of prestrung pearls around outside edge as shown.❀

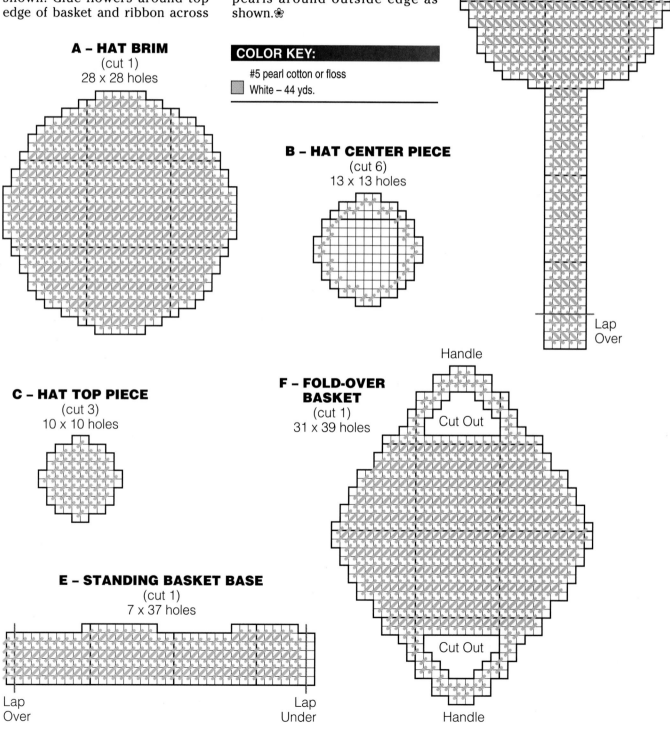

D – OPEN BASKET & STANDING BASKET TOP
(cut 1 each)
25 x 57 holes

Lap Under

Lap Over

A – HAT BRIM
(cut 1)
28 x 28 holes

B – HAT CENTER PIECE
(cut 6)
13 x 13 holes

C – HAT TOP PIECE
(cut 3)
10 x 10 holes

F – FOLD-OVER BASKET
(cut 1)
31 x 39 holes

Handle

Cut Out

Cut Out

Handle

E – STANDING BASKET BASE
(cut 1)
7 x 37 holes

Lap Over

Lap Under

ROSES & LACE

BY MICHELE WILCOX

Set a feminine tone for your bed and bath decor with a ribbon-trimmed tissue cover, vase and frame. Why not surprise Mom on Mother's Day with this pretty, lacy trio? The frame holds a 5" x 7" mirror or photo.

Instructions begin on page 24

23

SIZE: Tissue cover loosely covers a 5½"-tall boutique-style tissue box; Vase is 7½" x 7½" x 5¾" tall; Frame is 8" x 9¾" and holds a 5" x 7" mirror or photo.

SKILL LEVEL: Average

MATERIALS: Six sheets of 7-count plastic canvas; 3½ yds. pink 1¼" embossed satin ribbon; 2" sawtooth hanger (optional); Velcro® closure (optional); Craft glue or glue gun; Worsted-weight or plastic canvas yarn (for amounts see Color Key).

CUTTING INSTRUCTIONS:

A: For Tissue Cover sides, cut four according to graph.

B: For Tissue Cover top, cut one according to graph.

C: For optional Tissue Cover bottom and flap, cut one 31 x 31 holes and one 12 x 31 holes.

D: For Vase sides, cut four according to graph.

E: For Vase bottom, cut one 27 x 27 holes.

F: For Frame front, cut one according to graph.

G: For Frame back, cut one 52 x 64 holes.

H: For optional Frame stand, cut one 16 x 25 holes and one 16 x 45 holes.

STITCHING INSTRUCTIONS:

1: Using colors and stitches indicated, work A, B, D and F pieces according to graphs. Fill in uncoded areas and work E (bottom may be left unworked if desired) using White and Continental Stitch. With White, Overcast unfinished cutout edges.

NOTE: Cut ribbon into one 1-yd. and two 1¼-yd. lengths.

2: For Tissue Cover, with White, Whipstitch A and B pieces together. For optional bottom, Whipstitch C pieces together at one matching edge according to Tissue Cover Assembly Diagram. Whipstitch opposite edge of bottom to one side of cover. Overcast remaining unfinished bottom edges of cover. If desired, glue closure to flap and inside of cover. Starting at one corner, weave one 1¼-yd. ribbon through side cutouts as shown in photo; tie into a bow and trim ends.

3: For Vase, with White, Whipstitch side edges of D pieces together as indicated on graph; Whipstitch sides and E together. Overcast unfinished top edges of vase. Starting at one corner, weave remaining 1¼-yd. ribbon through side cutouts as shown in photo; tie into a bow and trim ends.

4: For Frame, if desired for optional stand, Whipstitch unworked H pieces together at one matching short edge; Whipstitch opposite edge of long H piece to unworked G centered along 22nd bar from top edge. Holding G and F wrong sides together, with White, Whipstitch together (if used, catch end of short H piece in seam at center bottom) as indicated on graph, leaving center top unjoined. Overcast unfinished edges. Tack front and back together as indicated. Starting at second cutout from upper left corner of front, weave 1-yd. ribbon through cutout at left; pull ribbon flat across back. Continue to weave from right to left through cutouts on front; tie into a bow and trim ends. Glue ribbon to center back of frame (hold front and back apart until glue dries). For hanging Frame, glue sawtooth hanger to ribbon.❀

F – FRAME FRONT
(cut 1)
52 x 64 holes

Whipstitch between arrows.

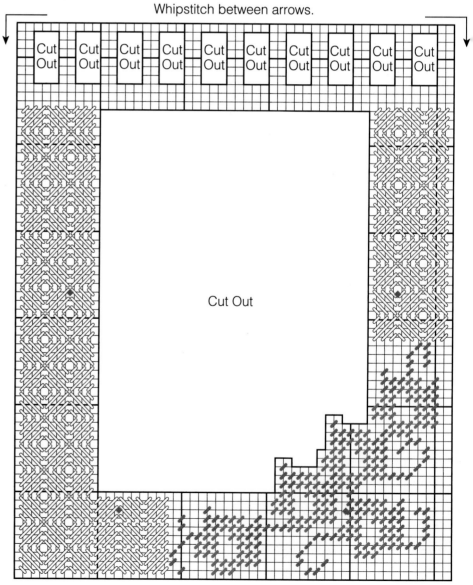

A – TISSUE COVER SIDE
(cut 4)
31 x 36 holes

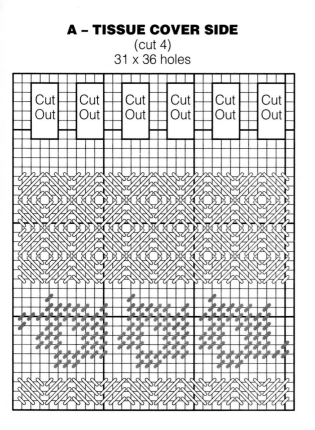

B – TISSUE COVER TOP
(cut 1)
31 x 31 holes

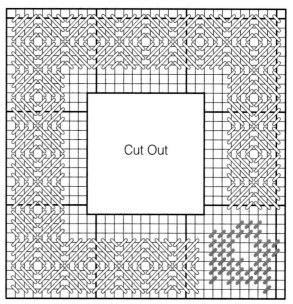

Cut Out

TISSUE COVER ASSEMBLY DIAGRAM

TISSUE COVER SIDE

Whipstitch here.

BOTTOM

FLAP

Whipstitch here.

D – VASE SIDE
(cut 4)
45 x 49 holes

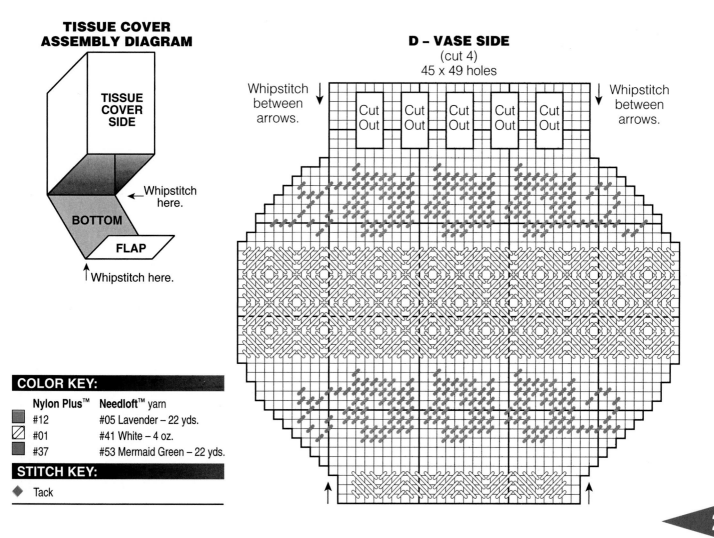

Whipstitch between arrows.

Whipstitch between arrows.

COLOR KEY:

Nylon Plus™	Needloft™ yarn	
#12	#05 Lavender – 22 yds.	
#01	#41 White – 4 oz.	
#37	#53 Mermaid Green – 22 yds.	

STITCH KEY:

◆ Tack

25

Climbing blossoms twine around this lofty residence for a fresh country accent that says "Home Sweet Home." This perky wreath brightens a room like a ray of April sunshine.

A COUNTRY BIRDHOUSE WREATH

BY MICHELE WILCOX

A – WREATH INSERT
(cut 1) 70 x 70 holes

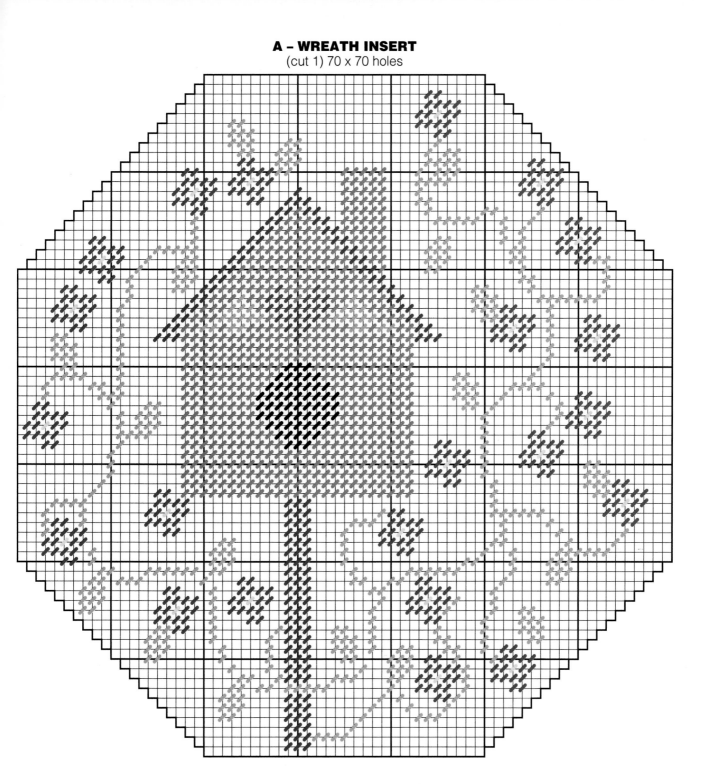

SIZE: Worked piece is 10½" x 10½".

SKILL LEVEL: Easy

MATERIALS: One sheet of 7-count plastic canvas; 14" grape-vine wreath; Artificial bird; Craft glue or glue gun; Worsted-weight or plastic canvas yarn (for amounts see Color Key).

CUTTING INSTRUCTIONS:
A: For wreath insert, cut one according to graph.

STITCHING INSTRUCTIONS:
1: Using colors indicated and Continental Stitch, work A according to graph. Fill in uncoded areas using Baby Blue and Continental Stitch. Do not Overcast unfinished edges.

2: Glue insert to back and bird to bottom front of wreath as shown in photo.✿

SIZE: Loosely covers a 4¾"-tall boutique-style tissue box.

SKILL LEVEL: Average

MATERIALS: Two sheets of 7-count plastic canvas; Eight 7-mm. wiggle eyes; Two gold ¾" safety pins; Velcro® closure (optional); Craft glue or glue gun; Worsted-weight or plastic canvas yarn (for amounts see Color Key).

CUTTING INSTRUCTIONS:

A: For top, cut one according to graph.

B: For sides, cut four 31 x 34 holes.

C: For optional cover bottom and flap, cut one 31 x 31 holes and one 12 x 31 holes.

D: For girl heads, cut two according to graph.

E: For boy heads, cut two according to graph.

F: For bodies, cut four according to graph.

G: For straight legs, cut four according to graph.

H: For bent legs, cut four according to graph.

cording to graph.

I: For arms, cut eight according to graph.

J: For skirts, cut two according to graph.

STITCHING INSTRUCTIONS:

1: For cover, using Lilac and stitches indicated, work A according to graph; Overcast unfinished cutout edges. Using Sail Blue, Lemon, Pink and Baby Green, work one B piece in each color according to Side Stitch Pattern Guide.

BUSY BABIES

BY SANDRA MILLER-MAXFIELD

I t's always nice to keep tissues handy in the nursery. Bouncing baby boys and pony-tailed baby girls frolic around this pastel, easy-to-stitch boutique tissue cover.

With Lilac, Whipstitch A and B pieces together, forming cover. For optional bottom, with Lilac, Whipstitch unworked C pieces together at one matching edge according to Tissue Cover Assembly Diagram on page 25. Whipstitch opposite edge of bottom to one side of cover. Overcast remaining unfinished bottom edges of cover. If desired, glue closure to flap and inside of cover.

2: For heads, using Lemon and stitches indicated, work one D piece according to graph. Substituting Sundown for Lemon, work remaining D according to graph. Fill in uncoded areas and work E pieces using Flesh Tone and Continental Stitch. Using Watermelon and Straight Stitch for mouths and Flesh Tone and French Knot for noses, embroider as indicated on graphs. With matching colors, Overcast unfinished edges of heads. Using Maple and Straight Stitch, embroider hair on one E as indicated.

3: For bodies, using colors and stitches indicated, work one F piece according to graph. Substituting Sail Blue, Watermelon and Lemon for Purple, work one F piece in each color according to graph. With matching colors, Overcast unfinished edges.

4: For legs and arms, using Sail Blue and stitches indicated, work two G and two I pieces according to graphs. Substituting Lemon for Sail Blue, work remaining G and two I pieces according to graphs. Using Purple and stitches indicated, work

two H pieces according to graph. Substituting Watermelon for Purple, work remaining H pieces according to graph. Substituting Watermelon and Purple for Sail Blue, work two I pieces in each color according to graph. Fill in uncoded areas of legs and arms using Flesh Tone and Continental Stitch. Using matching sock color and French Knot, embroider detail on straight legs as indicated. With matching colors, Overcast unfinished edges.

5: For skirts, using Purple and stitches indicated, work one J piece according to graph. Substituting Watermelon for Purple, work remaining J according to graph. With White for hem edges as indicated and with matching colors, Overcast unfinished edges.

NOTE: Cut two 9" lengths of Purple.

6: Tie each 9" length of Purple into a bow around one pigtail of red-headed girl. Secure one safety pin through each boy's diaper as shown in photo. Glue eyes to heads and matching color pieces together and to cover as shown.✿

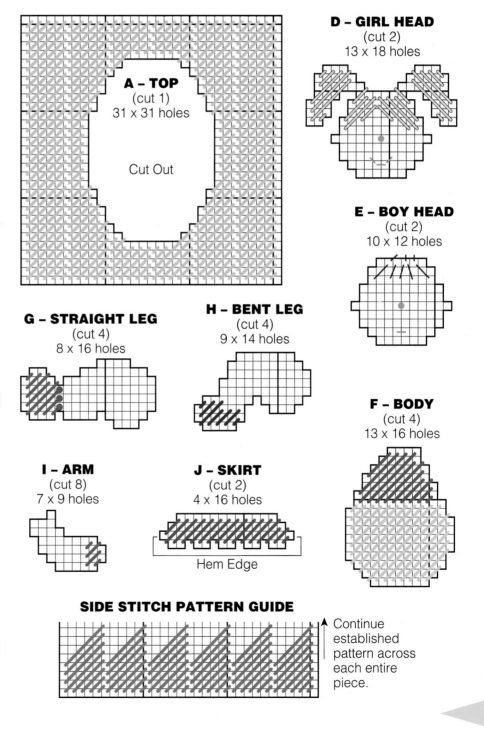

A – TOP
(cut 1)
31 x 31 holes

Cut Out

D – GIRL HEAD
(cut 2)
13 x 18 holes

E – BOY HEAD
(cut 2)
10 x 12 holes

G – STRAIGHT LEG
(cut 4)
8 x 16 holes

H – BENT LEG
(cut 4)
9 x 14 holes

F – BODY
(cut 4)
13 x 16 holes

I – ARM
(cut 8)
7 x 9 holes

J – SKIRT
(cut 2)
4 x 16 holes

Hem Edge

SIDE STITCH PATTERN GUIDE

Continue established pattern across each entire piece.

COLOR KEY:

	Nylon Plus™	Needloft™ yarn
	#11	#07 Pink – 14 yds.
	#16	#10 Sundown – 3 yds.
	#35	#13 Maple – 1/2 yd.
	#25	#20 Lemon – 20 yds.
	#28	#26 Baby Green – 14 yds.
	#04	#35 Sail Blue – 17 yds.
	#01	#41 White – 15 yds.
	#22	#45 Lilac – 24 yds.
	#21	#46 Purple – 6 yds.
	#54	#55 Watermelon – 6 yds.
	#14	#56 Flesh Tone – 40 yds.
	Side Color	

STITCH KEY:

— Backstitch/Straight Stitch
● French Knot

Your favorite toddler will love this colorful, educational book. She'll learn to zip the smiling clown's mouth, tie the tennis shoe and attach the flower to the stem. And – surprise! – add a music button and she'll hear a happy tune when she presses the heart's nose.

BY TINA MAXFIELD-RODGERS & SANDRA MILLER-MAXFIELD

MY CAN-DO BOOK

SIZE: 4⅝" x 5¾".

SKILL LEVEL: Average

MATERIALS: Three sheets of 7-count plastic canvas; Music button of choice and music button spacer; Velcro® closure; Short red nylon zipper; Three silver ball key chains; Sewing needle, red and white thread; Craft glue or glue gun; Worsted-weight or plastic canvas yarn (for amounts see Color Key).

CUTTING INSTRUCTIONS:

(See graphs on pages 32 & 33.)

A: For front and back covers and flower, heart, shoe and clown pages, cut one each according to graphs.

B: For sunglasses, cut one according to graph.

C: For nose, cut one according to graph.

D: For mouth, cut one according to graph.

E: For flower petals, cut one according to graph.

F: For flower center, cut one according to graph.

STITCHING INSTRUCTIONS:

1: Using colors and stitches indicated, work A, B, C, E (leave uncoded area unworked) and F pieces according to graphs. With Christmas Red for mouth, Watermelon for sunglasses and with matching colors, Overcast unfinished edges of B-F pieces. With Christmas Red, Overcast unfinished cutout edges of mouth on clown A.

2: Beginning at upper left corner of shoe and leaving about 6" of yarn hanging on front, using White and Straight Stitch, embroider laces on shoe A as indicated on graph, ending at upper right corner. Tie ends of laces into a bow; knot and trim ends.

3: Using Pumpkin and Modified Turkey Work (see Stitch Illustration), embroider hair on clown A as indicated. With white thread, sew fuzzy side of closure to flower A at top of stem and loopy side to

wrong side of E. Holding right side of zipper to wrong side of clown A, with red thread, sew zipper to stitches bordering mouth cutout.

4: Glue spacer and music button to wrong side of heart A behind nose area (see photo). Glue sunglasses, nose and mouth to heart as shown. Glue flower center to center of petals.

5: To join A pieces, holding front cover and heart A wrong sides

together, with Holly, Whipstitch cutout and outside edges together. With Watermelon, repeat with flower and shoe pages. With Royal, repeat with clown page and back cover.

6: Thread and secure one chain through matching cutouts on each joined page. Attach flower petals to closure on flower page. To activate music button, press nose on heart.❀

A – FRONT COVER (cut 1) 30 x 37 holes

Cut Out

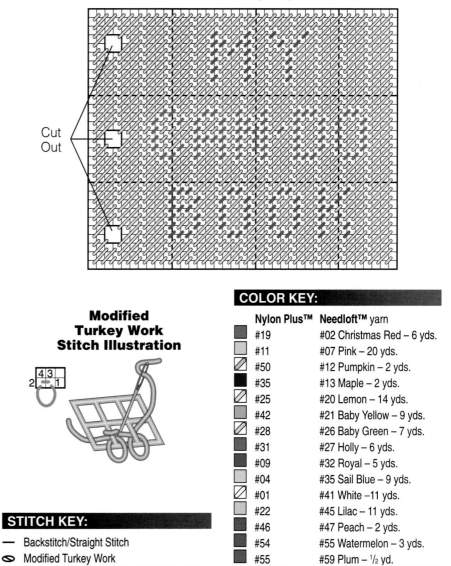

Modified Turkey Work Stitch Illustration

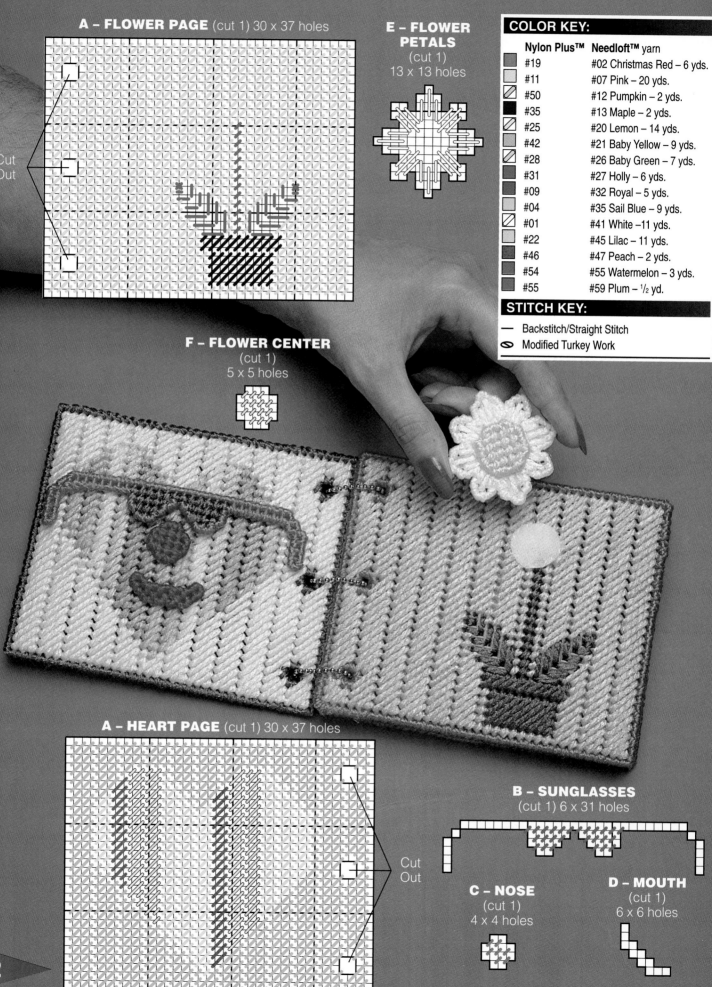

A – FLOWER PAGE (cut 1) 30 x 37 holes

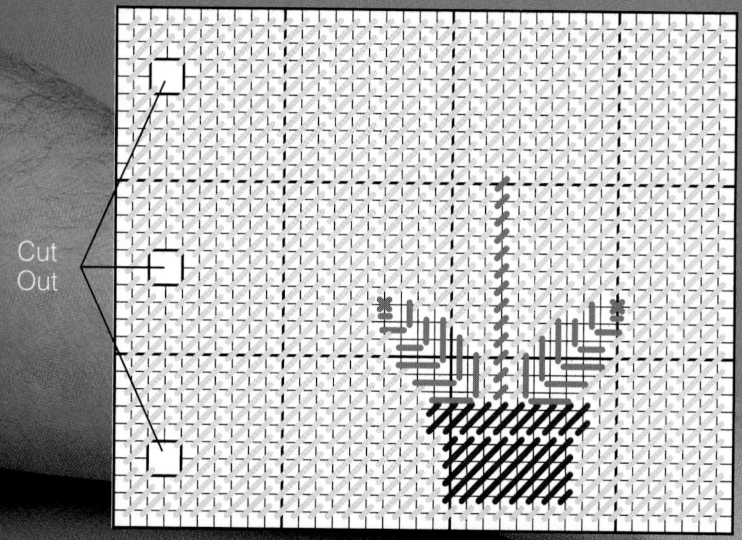
Cut
Out

E – FLOWER PETALS
(cut 1)
13 x 13 holes

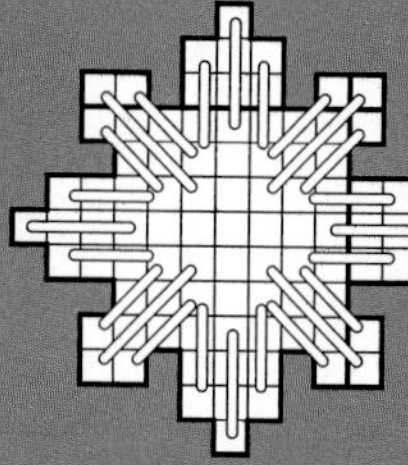

COLOR KEY:

	Nylon Plus™	Needloft™ yarn
	#19	#02 Christmas Red – 6 yds.
	#11	#07 Pink – 20 yds.
	#50	#12 Pumpkin – 2 yds.
	#35	#13 Maple – 2 yds.
	#25	#20 Lemon – 14 yds.
	#42	#21 Baby Yellow – 9 yds.
	#28	#26 Baby Green – 7 yds.
	#31	#27 Holly – 6 yds.
	#09	#32 Royal – 5 yds.
	#04	#35 Sail Blue – 9 yds.
	#01	#41 White –11 yds.
	#22	#45 Lilac – 11 yds.
	#46	#47 Peach – 2 yds.
	#54	#55 Watermelon – 3 yds.
	#55	#59 Plum – 1/2 yd.

STITCH KEY:

— Backstitch/Straight Stitch

⊘ Modified Turkey Work

F – FLOWER CENTER
(cut 1)
5 x 5 holes

A – HEART PAGE (cut 1) 30 x 37 holes

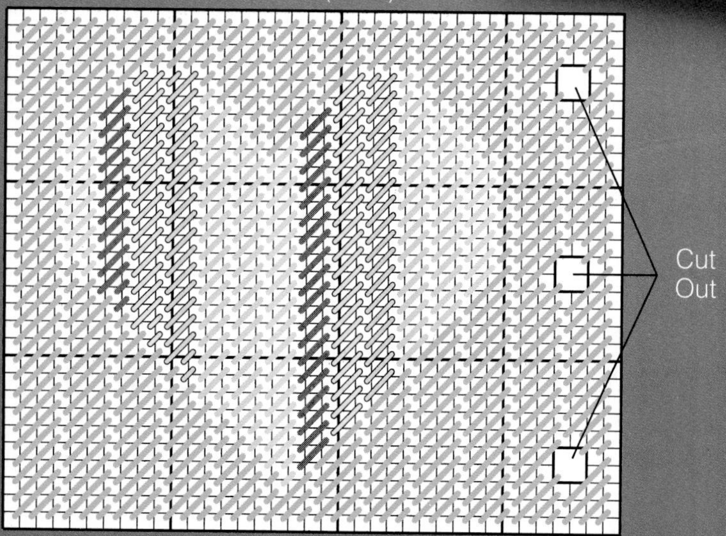
Cut
Out

B – SUNGLASSES
(cut 1) 6 x 31 holes

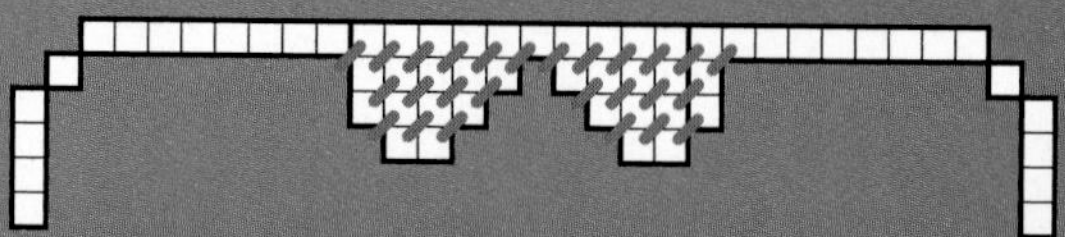

C – NOSE
(cut 1)
4 x 4 holes

D – MOUTH
(cut 1)
6 x 6 holes

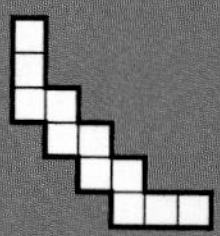

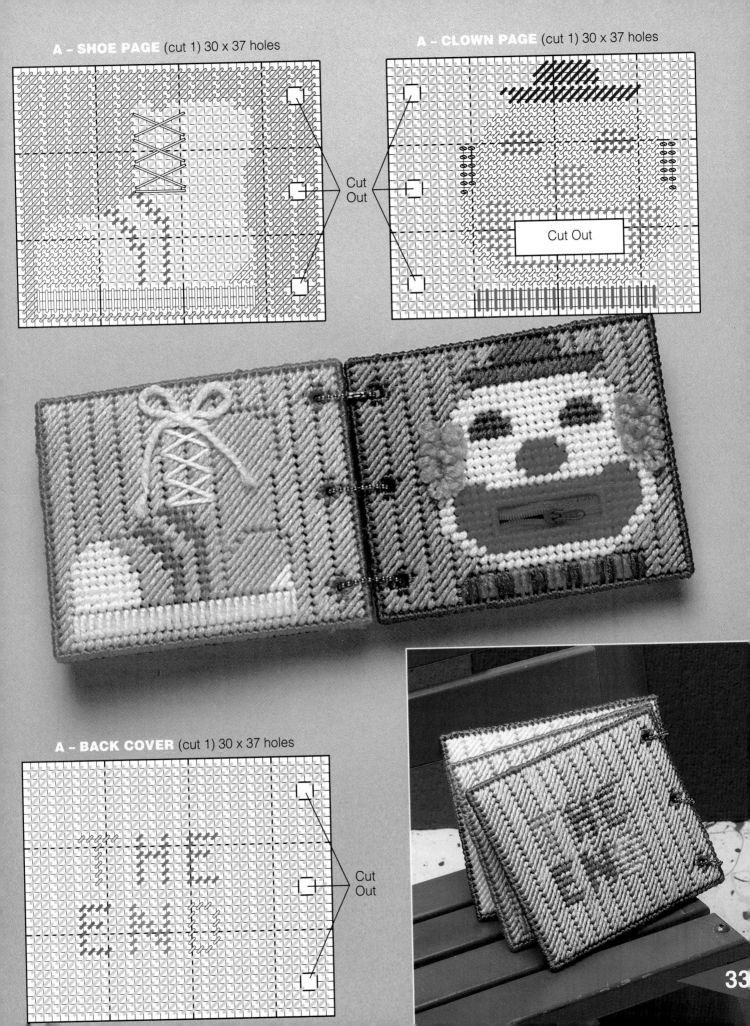

A – SHOE PAGE (cut 1) 30 x 37 holes

A – CLOWN PAGE (cut 1) 30 x 37 holes

Cut Out

Cut Out

A – BACK COVER (cut 1) 30 x 37 holes

Cut Out

33

Thank your child's dedicated teacher at the end of the year with a gift of this precious wall grouping. Mary lovingly scolds her little lamb and sends him back home.

SCHOOL

MARY
HAD A LITTLE LAMB

BY MICHELE WILCOX

SIZE: Mary is 7" x 9¼" tall, not including hair; Little Lamb is 5⅜" x 5¾" tall; School is 4¾" x 7¼" tall.

SKILL LEVEL: Easy

MATERIALS: Two sheets of 7-count plastic canvas; ½ yd. country blue ⅛" satin ribbon; Gold ¼" jingle bell; Sandy blonde doll hair; Three 1½" sawtooth hangers; Craft glue or glue gun; Worsted-weight or plastic canvas yarn (for amounts see Color Key).

CUTTING INSTRUCTIONS:

A: For Mary, cut two according to graph.

B: For Little Lamb, cut two according to graph.

C: For School, cut two according to graph.

STITCHING INSTRUCTIONS:

1: Using colors indicated and Continental Stitch, work one of each A, B and C pieces according to graphs. Fill in uncoded areas of A and B using White and C using Crimson and Continental Stitch.

2: Using Black for Mary's eye, Cerulean for Little Lamb's eye, Crimson for doorknob and French Knot, embroider as indicated on graph. Using Crimson and Straight Stitch, embroider cheek area of Mary's mouth as indicated.

3: Holding unworked pieces to wrong sides of matching worked pieces, with Black for angled edges of lower roof, Crimson for bottom edge of School and with matching colors, Whipstitch together. Using Crimson and Straight Stitch, embroider Mary's mouth as indicated.

NOTE: Cut ribbon into two 9" lengths.

4: Thread bell onto one ribbon; tie into a bow and trim ends. Glue to Little Lamb's head as shown in photo. Tie remaining ribbon into a bow; trim ends. Glue doll hair to Mary's head and bow to hair as shown. Glue one sawtooth hanger to center back of each piece.❀

COLOR KEY:

	Nylon Plus™	Needloft™ yarn
■	#02	#00 Black – 9 yds.
▨	#38	#34 Cerulean – 12 yds.
▨	#01	#41 White – 20 yds.
▨	#53	#42 Crimson – 13 yds.
▨	#14	#56 Flesh Tone – 11 yds.
▨	#26	#57 Yellow – 1 yd.

STITCH KEY:

— Backstitch/Straight Stitch

● French Knot

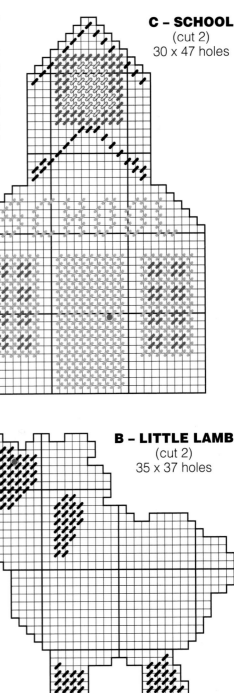

C – SCHOOL
(cut 2)
30 x 47 holes

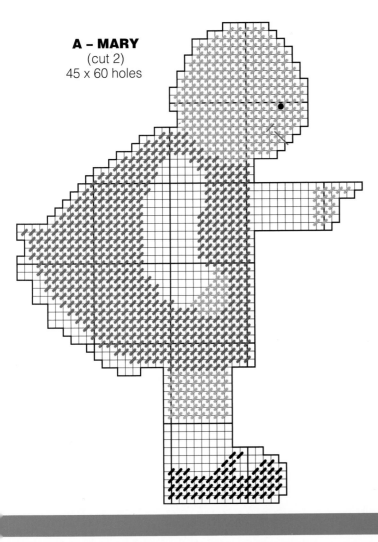

A – MARY
(cut 2)
45 x 60 holes

B – LITTLE LAMB
(cut 2)
35 x 37 holes

Decorate the nursery with this cheerful, lace-trimmed sampler and handy bunny basket. Baby will love the bright, coloring-book images.

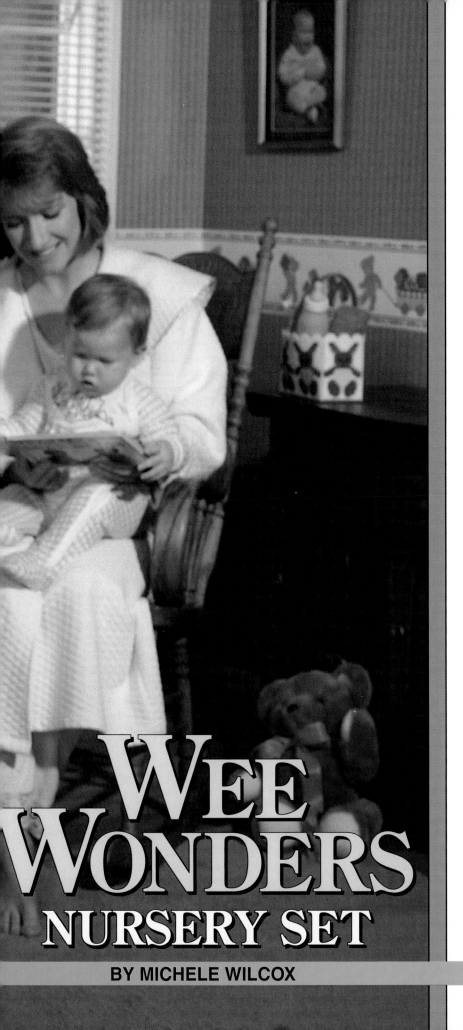

WEE WONDERS NURSERY SET

SIZE: Sampler is 9¾" x 12⅞", not including ruffle; Basket is 3¼" x 6½" x 4¾" tall, not including handle.

SKILL LEVEL: Easy

MATERIALS: Two sheets of 7-count plastic canvas; 1¼ yds. lt. blue 1⅜" eyelet ruffle; 2" sawtooth hanger; Craft glue or glue gun; #3 pearl cotton or six-strand embroidery floss (for amount see Color Key on page 38); Worsted-weight or plastic canvas yarn (for amounts see Color Key).

CUTTING INSTRUCTIONS:
(See graphs on pages 38 & 39.)

A: For Sampler, cut one 64 x 85 holes.

B: For Basket sides, cut two according to graph.

C: For Basket ends, cut two according to graph.

D: For Basket bottom, cut one 21 x 42 holes.

E: For Basket handle, cut one 4 x 84 holes.

STITCHING INSTRUCTIONS:

1: Using colors indicated and Continental Stitch, work A, one B and one C piece according to graphs. Substituting Watermelon for Lilac, Royal for Moss and Bright Orange for Yellow, work remaining B and C pieces according to graphs. Fill in uncoded areas using White and Continental Stitch. Using Watermelon and Continental Stitch, work D (bottom may be left unworked if desired) and E pieces; Overcast unfinished edges of A and E pieces.

2: Using pearl cotton or six strands floss, French Knot for eyes and Straight Stitch for noses and mouths, embroider as indicated on graphs.

3: For Basket, with White for side edges and Watermelon for bottom edges, Whipstitch B-D pieces together. With White, Overcast unfinished edges. Glue short ends of handle to sides of Basket as shown in photo.

4: For Sampler, glue ruffle around A as shown. Glue sawtooth hanger to center top of back.❈

Take these adorable diapered bunnies along on quick trips or use in the nursery to hold diapers, bottles or other items.

C – BASKET END
(cut 2)
21 x 30 holes

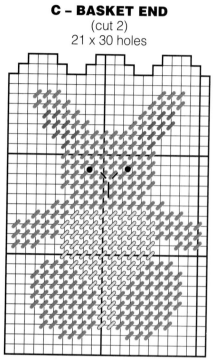

COLOR KEY:

#3 pearl cotton or floss
■ Black – 2 yds.

Nylon Plus™	Needloft™ yarn
#51	#09 Rust – 2½ yds.
#48	#25 Moss – 5 yds.
#09	#32 Royal – 5 yds.
#40	#37 Silver – 2 yds.
#01	#41 White– 60 yds.
#34	#43 Camel – 28 yds.
#22	#45 Lilac – 5 yds.
#54	#55 Watermelon – 40 yds.
#26	#57 Yellow – 5 yds.
#17	#58 Bright Orange – 2 yds.

STITCH KEY:

— Backstitch/Straight Stitch
● French Knot

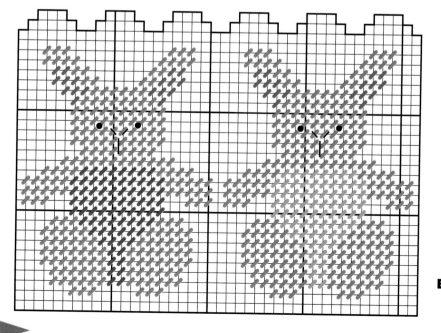

B – BASKET SIDE
(cut 2)
30 x 42 holes

A – SAMPLER
(cut 1)
64 x 85 holes

BY MICHELE WILCOX

LET'S GO BYE-BYE!

Roomy enough to carry baby's things for an afternoon outing, this whimsical bag sports a cute baby holding all of his favorite things.

SIZE: 4⅝" x 9⅛" x 7¾" tall, not including handles.

SKILL LEVEL: Easy

MATERIALS: 2½ sheets of 7-count plastic canvas; Worsted-weight or plastic canvas yarn (for amounts see Color Key).

CUTTING INSTRUCTIONS:

A: For front and back, cut one each 50 x 60 holes.

B: For ends, cut two 30 x 50 holes.

C: For bottom, cut one 30 x 60 holes.

D: For handles, cut two 6 x 86 holes.

STITCHING INSTRUCTIONS:

1: Using colors and stitches indicated, work front A and B pieces according to graphs. Fill in uncoded areas on front A using Baby Green and Continental Stitch. Using Royal and French Knot for eyes and Watermelon, French Knot and Straight Stitch for nose and mouths, embroider as indicated on graph. Following pattern estab-lished on ends, work back A and C (bottom may be left unworked if desired). Using White and Scotch Stitch over 5 bars, work D pieces. With Baby Green, Overcast un-finished long edges of handles.

2: With Baby Green, Whipstitch A-C pieces together, forming tote. Overcast unfinished edges, catching short ends of handles at front and back to join as indicated and as shown in photo.✿

COLOR KEY:

Nylon Plus™	Needloft™ yarn
#44	#14 Cinnamon – 5 yds.
#28	#26 Baby Green – 62 yds.
#09	#32 Royal – 3½ yds.
#01	#41 White – 45 yds.
#54	#55 Watermelon – 1 yd.
#14	#56 Flesh Tone – 36 yds.
#26	#57 Yellow – ½ yd.

STITCH KEY:

—	Backstitch/Straight Stitch
●	French Knot

B – END
(cut 2) 30 x 50 holes

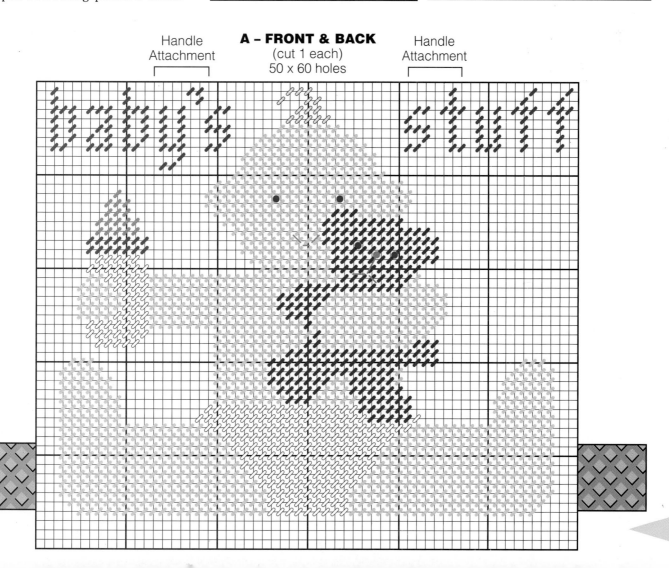

Handle Attachment

A – FRONT & BACK
(cut 1 each)
50 x 60 holes

Handle Attachment

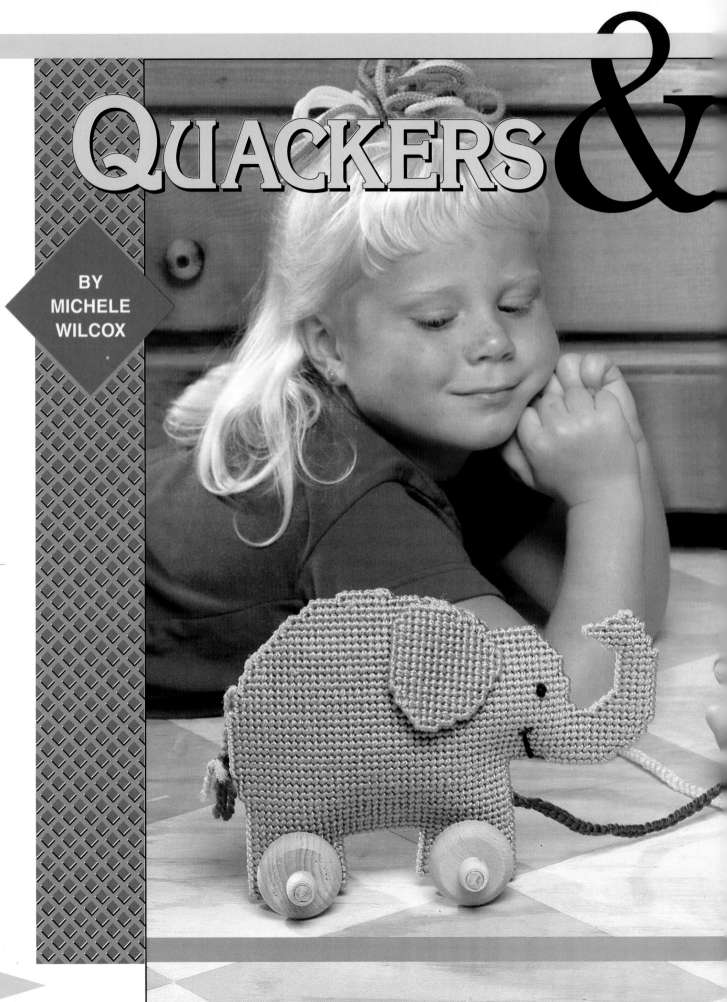

QUACKERS &

BY
MICHELE
WILCOX

PEANUTS

These fun and friendly pets will roll merrily into your child's world, bringing along lots of grins and giggles. Wooden wheels and axles are easily attached for smooth rolling and good times aplenty.

Instructions begin on page 44

SIZE: Elephant is 9" x 6½" tall; Duck is 7½" x 7¼" tall.

MATERIALS: Two sheets of 7-count plastic canvas; Four 4" lengths of ⅜" dowel; Eight ⅝" wooden barrel beads; Eight 1¾" wooden wheels; ¾ yd. of 1¼" ribbon; Polyester fiberfill; Craft glue or glue gun; Wood glue; Worsted-weight or plastic canvas yarn (for amounts see Color Key).

CUTTING INSTRUCTIONS:

A: For Elephant and Duck bodies, cut two each according to graphs.

B: For Elephant ears, cut two according to graph.

C: For Duck wings, cut two according to graph.

STITCHING INSTRUCTIONS:

1: Using colors indicated and Continental Stitch, work A and B pieces (one of each) on opposite sides of canvas, according to graphs. Using Black and French Knot for eyes and Straight Stitch for mouth, embroider Elephant as indicated on graph. With matching colors, Overcast unfinished edges of B and C pieces and unfinished

cutout edges of A pieces.

NOTE: Cut three 7" lengths of Silver and one 10" length of Burgundy.

2: For Elephant's tail, tie 7" lengths of Silver together in knot close to one end. For each body, holding matching A pieces wrong sides together and stuffing with fiberfill before closing, with matching colors, Whipstitch together, inserting knotted end of Elephant's tail between body pieces as indicated as you work.

3: Glue wings and ears to bodies as indicated. Tie ribbon into a bow around Duck's neck as shown in photo. Braid strands of tail about 2" and tie ends in knot; trim ends to ¾". Tie 10" length of Burgundy into a bow around knot as shown.

4: For each toy, insert one dowel through each cutout on body; place wheels on dowels and glue one bead to each end to secure.

NOTE: Cut three 1-yd. lengths each of Lemon and Burgundy.

5: For each pull cord, braid matching color lengths together; knot each end. Glue one end in a loop and opposite end to front of matching color toy as shown.❀

COLOR KEY:

Nylon Plus™	Needloft™ yarn
■ #02	#00 Black – 2 yds.
□ #13	#03 Burgundy – 3½ yds.
▨ #25	#20 Lemon – 72 yds.
▨ #40	#37 Silver – 72 yds.
▨ #17	#58 Bright Orange – 3 yds.

STITCH KEY:

— Backstitch/Straight Stitch
● French Knot
□ Ear/Wing Placement
◆ Tail Placement

B – ELEPHANT EAR
(cut 2)
15 x 16 holes

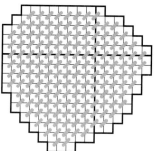

A – ELEPHANT BODY
(cut 2)
42 x 60 holes

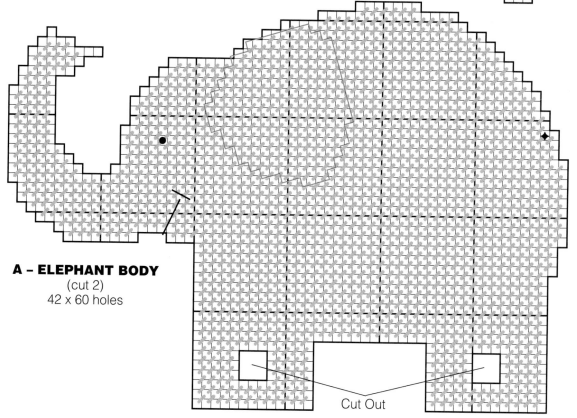

Cut Out

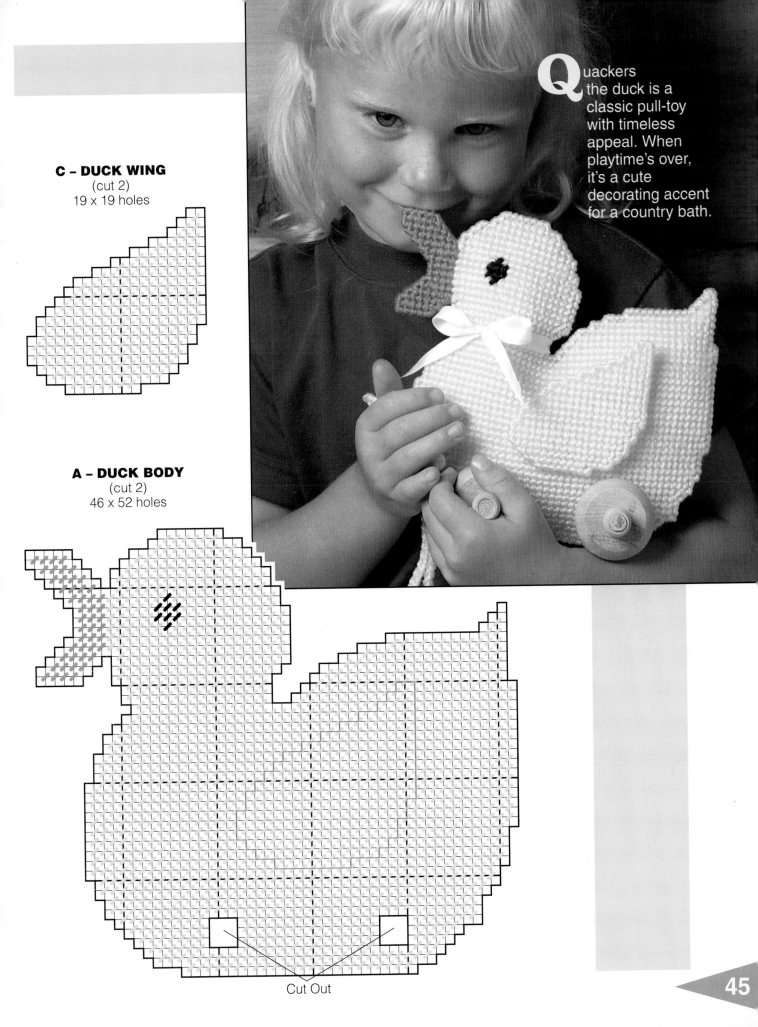

C – DUCK WING
(cut 2)
19 x 19 holes

A – DUCK BODY
(cut 2)
46 x 52 holes

Quackers the duck is a classic pull-toy with timeless appeal. When playtime's over, it's a cute decorating accent for a country bath.

Cut Out

S E A S O N A L

The Celebrations of Summer

Wispy clouds floating across an azure sky, juicy red watermelons and colorful garden blossoms — these are the gentle blessings of summer. It's a time for light and easy entertaining, honoring Dad on Father's Day, and brightening up your wardrobe and home decor with fresh, fun accents. ✳

SENSATIONS

TREE HOUSE ROOM SIGN

BY GINA WOODS

SIZE: 9⅜" x 12½", not including hanger.

SKILL LEVEL: Average

MATERIALS: 1¼ sheets of 7-count plastic canvas; Scraps of beige 7-count plastic canvas; Scraps of 10-count plastic canvas; ⅔ yd. tan 6-mm. braided macramé cord; Six-strand embroidery floss or tapestry wool (for amounts see Color Key on page 51); Worsted-weight or plastic canvas yarn (for amounts see Color Key).

CUTTING INSTRUCTIONS:

(See graphs on pages 50 and 51.)

NOTE: Use beige canvas for E pieces and 10-count canvas for G-K pieces.

A: For background, cut one 62 x 82 holes.

B: For tree house front, cut one according to graph.

C: For roof, cut one according to graph.

D: For porch, cut one according to graph.

E: For porch rails, cut two from beige according to graph.

F: For steps, cut three 1 x 6 holes.

G: For boy, cut one from 10-count according to graph.

H: For girl, cut one from 10-count according to graph.

I: For puppy, cut one from 10-count according to graph.

J: For puppy ear, cut one from 10-count according to graph.

K: For sign, cut one from 10-count 5 x 18 holes.

STITCHING INSTRUCTIONS:

1: Using Baby Blue and Continental Stitch, work child's name as indicated on A graph according to Alphabet Graph. Using yarn colors and stitches indicated, work remainder of A, B, C, D and F pieces according to graphs. Fill in uncoded areas of A using Holly and Continental Stitch.

2: Using six strands med. brown floss, Baby Blue yarn and Straight Stitch, embroider letter detail and outlines as indicated on Alphabet Graph. With matching colors, Overcast unfinished edges of A, C and F pieces and unfinished cutout edges of B.

3: With Sandstone, Whipstitch E pieces together at one matching short edge; Whipstitch B, D and porch rails together as indicated. Overcast remaining unfinished edges of B.

4: Using 12 strands floss in colors indicated and Continental Stitch, work G-J pieces according to graphs. Fill in uncoded areas of G-I pieces and work K using peach for boy and girl, white for puppy and sign and Continental Stitch. With dk. brown for hair edges of boy, yellow for hair edges of girl and with matching colors, Overcast unfinished edges of G, H, J and K pieces. With black for nose and spot areas as shown in photo and with matching colors, Overcast unfinished edges of I.

5: Using six strands floss in colors indicated, French Knot for eyes and dot on sign; Backstitch for mouths (use three strands for puppy's mouth) and puppy's leg outline; and Straight Stitch for boy's shirt, letters on sign and hair, embroider detail on G-I and K pieces as indicated.

NOTE: Cut eight 3" lengths of yellow floss and two 9" lengths of pink floss.

6: For girl's ponytails, holding two 3" lengths of yellow together, thread through one hole on side of head as indicated, pull ends to even; repeat in each indicated

hole. For ribbons, tie pink floss into a bow around each ponytail close to head; trim ends.

NOTE: Cut one 7" and one 16" length of macramé cord.

7: Reversing positions of boy and girl if desired, glue pieces together and to background as shown in photo. Knot one end of 7" cord to porch rail as shown. For hanger, thread ends of 16" cord from back to front at top of sign as indicated. Tie each end in knot; trim ends.✳

ALPHABET GRAPH

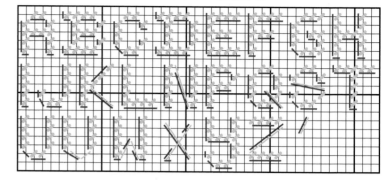

A – BACKGROUND (cut 1) 62 x 82 holes

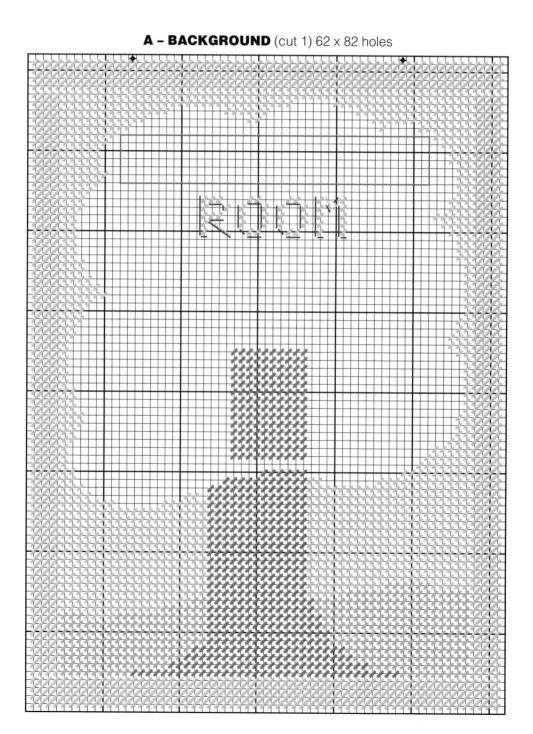

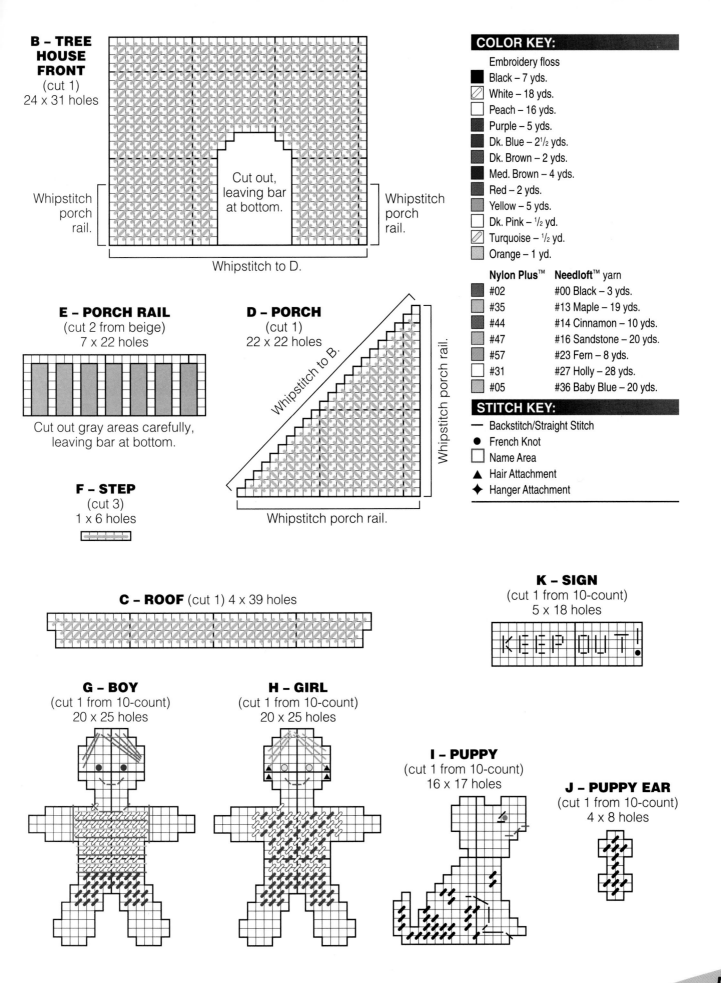

B – TREE HOUSE FRONT
(cut 1)
24 x 31 holes

Whipstitch porch rail.

Cut out, leaving bar at bottom.

Whipstitch porch rail.

Whipstitch to D.

E – PORCH RAIL
(cut 2 from beige)
7 x 22 holes

Cut out gray areas carefully, leaving bar at bottom.

D – PORCH
(cut 1)
22 x 22 holes

Whipstitch to B.

Whipstitch porch rail.

Whipstitch porch rail.

F – STEP
(cut 3)
1 x 6 holes

COLOR KEY:

Embroidery floss

■	Black – 7 yds.
▨	White – 18 yds.
□	Peach – 16 yds.
■	Purple – 5 yds.
■	Dk. Blue – 2½ yds.
■	Dk. Brown – 2 yds.
■	Med. Brown – 4 yds.
■	Red – 2 yds.
▨	Yellow – 5 yds.
□	Dk. Pink – ½ yd.
▨	Turquoise – ½ yd.
▨	Orange – 1 yd.

Nylon Plus™ Needloft™ yarn

■	#02	#00 Black – 3 yds.
▨	#35	#13 Maple – 19 yds.
■	#44	#14 Cinnamon – 10 yds.
▨	#47	#16 Sandstone – 20 yds.
■	#57	#23 Fern – 8 yds.
□	#31	#27 Holly – 28 yds.
▨	#05	#36 Baby Blue – 20 yds.

STITCH KEY:

— Backstitch/Straight Stitch
● French Knot
□ Name Area
▲ Hair Attachment
✦ Hanger Attachment

C – ROOF (cut 1) 4 x 39 holes

K – SIGN
(cut 1 from 10-count)
5 x 18 holes

KEEP OUT!

G – BOY
(cut 1 from 10-count)
20 x 25 holes

H – GIRL
(cut 1 from 10-count)
20 x 25 holes

I – PUPPY
(cut 1 from 10-count)
16 x 17 holes

J – PUPPY EAR
(cut 1 from 10-count)
4 x 8 holes

51

TAPESTRY ACCENTS

BY NIKI RUSSOS-ATKINSON

SIZE: Purse is 3⅝" x 13¾" x 10⅛" tall, not including handles; Key Ring is 3⅛" x 4⅛"; Eyeglasses Case is 4⅜" x 7"; Coupon Holder is 3⅝" x 8½"; Pen Holder is 2⅞" x 6¾".

SKILL LEVEL: Average

MATERIALS FOR ONE OF EACH: One sheet of 12" x 18" or larger 7-count plastic canvas; Three sheets of 7-count plastic canvas; 1½" split key ring; One black 9" x 12" felt square (optional); Worsted-weight or plastic canvas yarn (for amounts see Color Key on page 55).

CUTTING INSTRUCTIONS:
(See graphs on pages 54 and 55.)

NOTE: Use large sheet for B-G pieces.

A: For Purse sides, cut two according to graph.

B: For Purse end/bottom pieces, cut two 23 x 89 holes.

C: For Purse handles, cut two 5 x 120 holes.

D: For Purse button, cut one 4 x 4 holes.

E: For Key Ring, cut one according to graph.

F: For Eyeglasses Case sides, cut two 28 x 46 holes.

G: For Coupon Holder sides, cut two 23 x 56 holes.

H: For Pen Holder sides, cut two 18 x 44 holes.

I: For optional Eyeglasses Case lining, using F as a pattern, cut two from felt ⅛" smaller at all edges.

STITCHING INSTRUCTIONS:

1: For Purse, using colors indicated and Continental Stitch, work A pieces according to graph. Fill in uncoded areas and work B pieces using Red and Continental Stitch. Using Black and Continental Stitch, work C and D pieces; Overcast unfinished edges of handles and button.

NOTE: Cut one 8" length of Black.

2: With Red, Whipstitch B pieces together at one short end. Centering seam on bottom and easing to fit, Whipstitch long edges of end/bottom piece to sides as indicated on graph. With Red, Overcast unfinished top edges of Purse. Tack ends of one handle to wrong side of each side as indicated. Working over center stitch on button, with Black, tack button to one side as indicated. Thread ends of 8" strand of Black from front to back through side opposite button as indicated; tie ends in knot on wrong side, leaving a 2" loop on front to hook over button. Trim ends.

3: For accessories, using colors indicated and Continental Stitch, work E-H pieces according to graphs. Fill in uncoded areas using Black for E (leave indicated areas unworked) and F pieces, Red for G pieces and White for H pieces and Continental Stitch.

4: For Key Ring, with Black, Overcast unfinished edges of E as indicated. Folding E in half wrong sides together as indicated, Whipstitch unfinished edges and unworked areas together. Thread split ring on loop.

5: For Eyeglasses Case, if desired, glue one I to wrong side of each F. Holding F pieces wrong sides together, with Black, Whipstitch together, leaving one short end unjoined. For Pen Holder, Whipstitch H pieces together as for Eyeglasses Case. Overcast unfinished edges of Eyeglasses Case and Pen Holder.

6: For Coupon Holder, holding G pieces wrong sides together, with Black for border and with Red, Whipstitch together as indicated. With Black, Overcast unfinished edges.✳

E – KEY RING
(cut 1)
20 x 55 holes

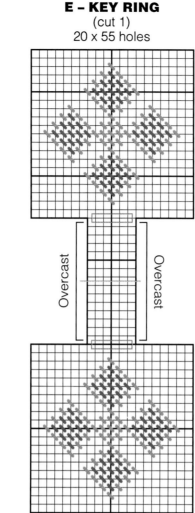

Overcast Overcast

G – COUPON HOLDER SIDE
(cut 2)
23 x 56 holes

Whipstitch between arrows. ←

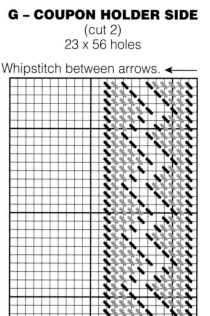
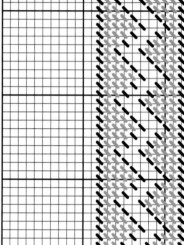

H – PEN HOLDER SIDE
(cut 2)
18 x 44 holes

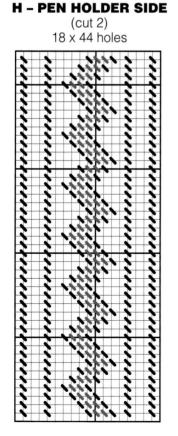

F – EYEGLASSES CASE SIDE
(cut 2)
28 x 46 holes

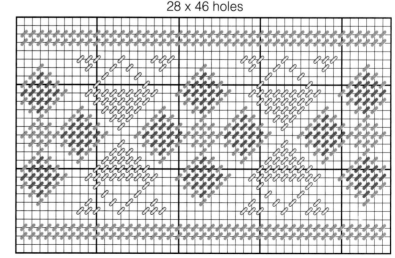

54

Whipstitch between arrows.

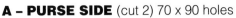

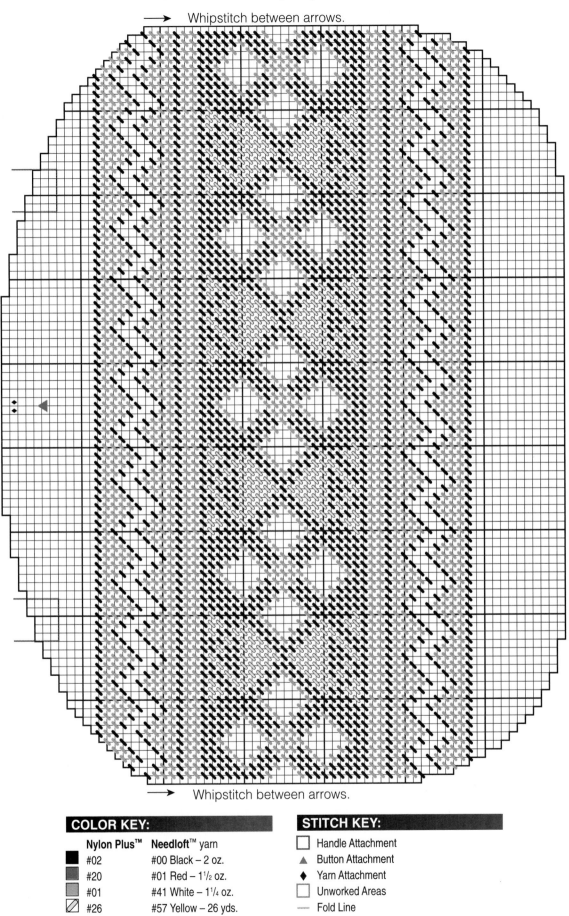

Whipstitch between arrows.

COLOR KEY:

Nylon Plus™	Needloft™ yarn
#02	#00 Black – 2 oz.
#20	#01 Red – 1½ oz.
#01	#41 White – 1¼ oz.
#26	#57 Yellow – 26 yds.

STITCH KEY:

☐ Handle Attachment
▲ Button Attachment
◆ Yarn Attachment
☐ Unworked Areas
— Fold Line

This colorful mallard is a tasteful accent in any season. Reminiscent of warm days spent fishing with Dad, it brings greetings of welcome to all your guests.

SIZE: 8" x about 9¾".
SKILL LEVEL: Easy
MATERIALS: Two sheets of 7-count plastic canvas; 2" sawtooth hanger; ⅓ yd. orange ⅛" satin ribbon; Craft glue or glue gun; Worsted-weight or plastic canvas yarn (for amounts see Color Key).

CUTTING INSTRUCTIONS:
A: For mallard, cut two according to graph.
B: For sign, cut two according to graph.

STITCHING INSTRUCTIONS:
1: Using colors indicated and Continental Stitch, work one of each A and B pieces according to graphs. Fill in uncoded areas of A using Cinnamon and B using Silver and Continental Stitch. Using Sundown and French Knot, embroider eye as indicated on graph.
2: Holding unworked piece to wrong side of matching worked piece, with matching colors for mallard and Sundown for sign, Whipstitch together. Tie ribbon into a bow around mallard's neck; trim ends.
NOTE: Cut two 6" lengths of Cinnamon.
3: Thread each 6" strand of Cinnamon through corresponding holes on each piece as indicated. Knot on wrong side; trim ends and glue to secure. Glue sawtooth hanger to wrong side of mallard. ☀

COUNTRY WELCOME SIGN

BY MICHELE WILCOX

A – MALLARD
(cut 2)
40 x 53 holes

B – SIGN
(cut 2)
14 x 52 holes

COLOR KEY:

	Nylon Plus™	Needloft™ yarn
	#16	#10 Sundown – 9 yds.
	#15	#11 Tangerine – 1½ yds.
	#44	#14 Cinnamon – 12 yds.
	#32	#29 Forest – 8 yds.
	#40	#37 Silver – 15 yds.
	#01	#41 White – ½ yd.

STITCH KEY:
● French Knot
✦ Hanger Placement

UNCLE SAM DOORSTOP

BY TRUDY BATH SMITH

SIZE: 2¾" x 4¼" x 17¾" tall.

SKILL LEVEL: Average

MATERIALS: Three sheets of 7-count plastic canvas; Brick or zip-close bag full of popcorn, dried beans or gravel; Velcro® closure; Craft glue or glue gun; Metallic cord (for amount see Color Key on page 61); Worsted-weight or plastic canvas yarn (for amounts see Color Key).

CUTTING INSTRUCTIONS:

(See graphs on pages 60 and 61.)

A: For front and back, cut one each 27 x 90 holes.

B: For sides, cut two 17 x 90 holes.

C: For arms, cut two according to graph.

D: For bottom, cut one 17 x 27 holes.

E: For bottom flap, cut one according to graph.

F: For hat brim, cut one according to graph.

G: For hat front and back, cut one each 25 x 27 holes.

H: For hat sides, cut two 17 x 25 holes.

I: For hat top, cut one 17 x 27 holes.

STITCHING INSTRUCTIONS:

1: Using colors and stitches indicated, work one A, B (work trousers stitch pattern in opposite direction on second piece), C (one on opposite side of canvas), one G and H pieces according to graphs. Fill in uncoded areas of B, C, G and H pieces and work F using Royal and Continental Stitch. Using Red and Continental Stitch, work I. Using Royal and Slanted Gobelin Stitch over 2 bars, work remaining A and G pieces in vertical rows. With matching colors, Overcast unfinished edges of arms and hat brim as indicated on graph.

2: Using Black and French Knot for eyes, Black for nose, Red for mouth and White for moustache and Straight Stitch, embroider as indicated on graph.

3: With matching colors, Whipstitch A and B pieces together as indicated, forming base. With Black, Whipstitch D and E pieces together at one matching edge. Whipstitch opposite edge of bottom to front of base. Overcast remaining unfinished bottom edges of base.

4: With Royal, Whipstitch inner edges of hat brim to top of base as shown in Hat Assembly Diagram. With matching colors, Whipstitch G-I pieces together, forming hat. With Royal, Overcast unfinished front and side edges of hat; Whipstitch hat and base together at unfinished edges of back. Glue front and sides of hat to brim and one arm to each side of base as shown in photo. Glue closure to bottom flap and inside of base. Place brick or other weight inside base.✳

A – FRONT
(cut 1)
27 x 90 holes

B – SIDE
(cut 2)
17 x 90 holes

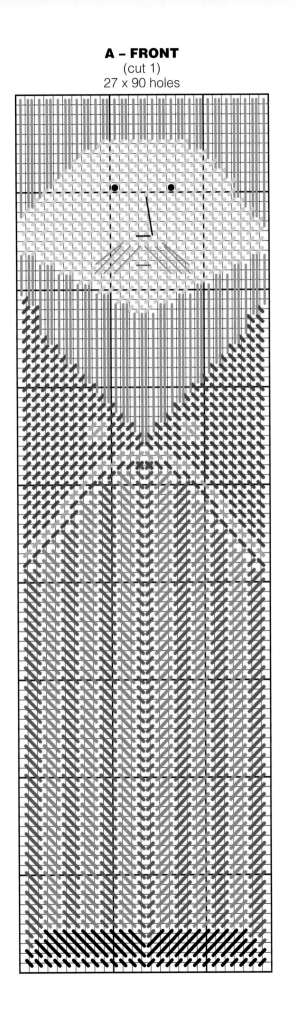

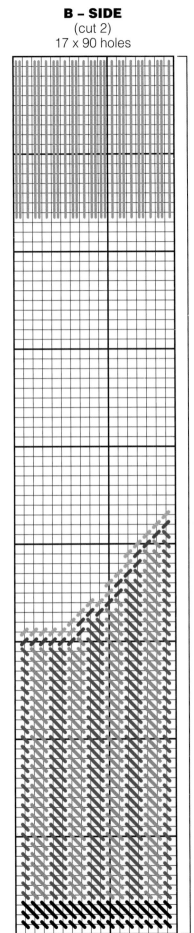

Whipstitch to front.

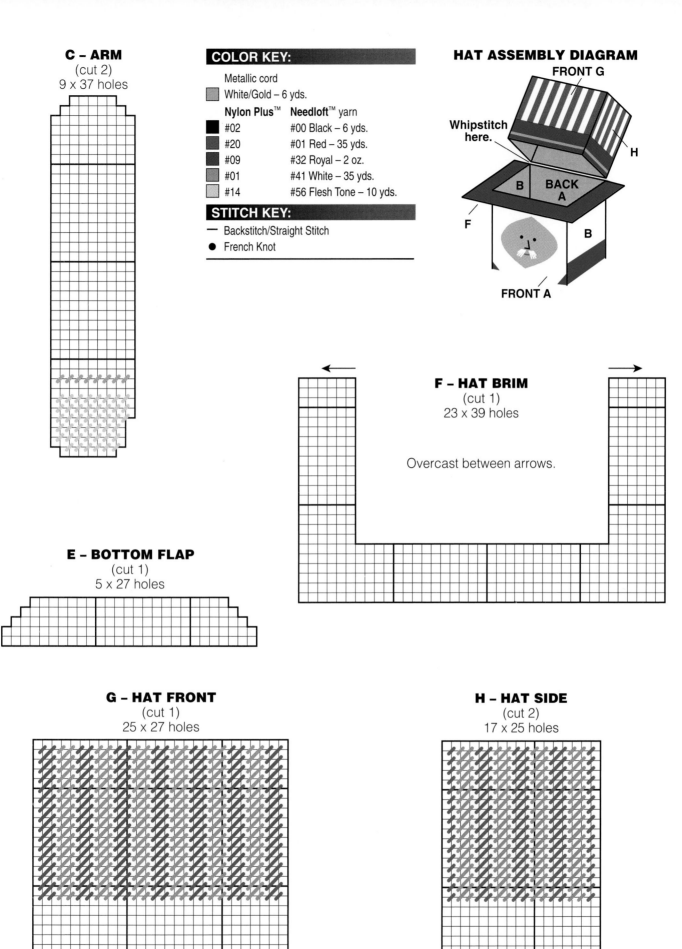

C – ARM
(cut 2)
9 x 37 holes

COLOR KEY:

Metallic cord
White/Gold – 6 yds.

Nylon Plus™	Needloft™ yarn
#02	#00 Black – 6 yds.
#20	#01 Red – 35 yds.
#09	#32 Royal – 2 oz.
#01	#41 White – 35 yds.
#14	#56 Flesh Tone – 10 yds.

STITCH KEY:
— Backstitch/Straight Stitch
● French Knot

HAT ASSEMBLY DIAGRAM

FRONT G

Whipstitch here.

H

B   BACK A

F   B

FRONT A

F – HAT BRIM
(cut 1)
23 x 39 holes

Overcast between arrows.

E – BOTTOM FLAP
(cut 1)
5 x 27 holes

G – HAT FRONT
(cut 1)
25 x 27 holes

H – HAT SIDE
(cut 2)
17 x 25 holes

61

DEER VALET

BY TERRY A. RICIOLI

Here's a gift that's sure to rack up lots of smiles from Dad on Father's Day — it will hold all his treasures and keep his dresser neat.

SIZE: 6¾" x 7⅜" x 3⅛" tall.

SKILL LEVEL: Easy

MATERIALS: Two sheets of 7-count plastic canvas; Two aqua 9" x 12" felt squares; Craft glue or glue gun; Six-strand embroidery floss (for amount see Color Key); Worsted-weight or plastic canvas yarn (for amounts see Color Key).

CUTTING INSTRUCTIONS:

A: For lid top, cut one 44 x 48 holes.

B: For lid short and long sides, cut two 6 x 44 holes and two 6 x 48 holes.

C: For box short and long sides, cut two 18 x 42 holes and two 18 x 46 holes.

D: For bottom, cut one 42 x 46 holes.

E: For lining, using A, C and D pieces as patterns, cut one each from felt ⅛" smaller at all edges.

STITCHING INSTRUCTIONS:

1: Using colors indicated and Continental Stitch, work A, short B and short C pieces according to graphs. Fill in uncoded areas and work D (**NOTE:** Bottom may be left unworked.) using Aqua and Continental Stitch. Following pattern established on short sides, work long B and C pieces. Using six strands floss and Backstitch, embroider outlines as indicated on graph.

2: With Aqua, Whipstitch C and D pieces together, forming box; Overcast unfinished edges. With Forest, Whipstitch A and B pieces together, forming lid; Overcast unfinished edges. Glue matching lining pieces inside box and lid.✳

A – LID TOP
(cut 1)
44 x 48 holes

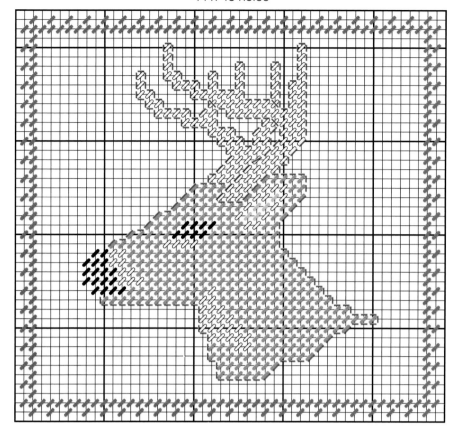

B – LID SHORT SIDE
(cut 2)
6 x 44 holes

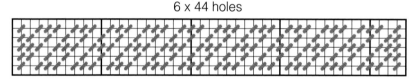

C – BOX SHORT SIDE
(cut 2)
18 x 42 holes

COLOR KEY:

Embroidery floss

	Dk. brown – 5 yds.

	Nylon Plus™	Needloft™ yarn
	#02	#00 Black – 1 yd.
	#44	#14 Cinnamon – small amount
	#32	#29 Forest – 46 yds.
◺	#43	#40 Beige – 5 yds.
	#34	#43 Camel – 6 yds.
	#60	#51 Aqua – 3 oz.

STITCH KEY:

— Backstitch/Straight Stitch

63

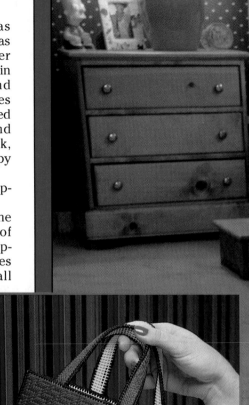

SIZE: Large Tote is 12" x 13½" x 11⅞" tall; Medium Tote is 9¼" x 10¾" x 9¾" tall; Small Tote is 6½" x 8¼" x 7½" tall, not including handles.

SKILL LEVEL: Challenging

MATERIALS: 16 sheets of 7-count plastic canvas; 10½ sheets of white 7-count plastic canvas; Two size 4 (15-mm.) snaps; Twelve 2" wooden wheels; 56" of ¼" wooden dowel; Wood glue; Craft glue or glue gun; Worsted-weight or plastic canvas yarn (for amounts see Color Key on page 67).

LARGE TOTE

CUTTING INSTRUCTIONS:

(See graphs on pages 66 and 67.)

NOTE: Use white canvas for tote lining pieces and pull handle lining pieces.

A: For tote sides and side linings, cut two from each color 70 x 87 holes.

B: For tote end pieces and end lining pieces, cut four from each color 33 x 70 holes.

C: For tote bottom and bottom lining, cut one from each color 66 x 87 holes.

D: For handles and handle linings, cut two from each color 5 x 70 holes.

E: For large puppy and butterfly motifs, cut one each according to graphs.

F: For base sides, cut four 10 x 89 holes; cut out axle opening at each end of each piece according to Base Side Cutting & Stitch Pattern Guide.

G: For base ends, cut four 10 x 68 holes.

H: For base bottom, cut one 68 x 89 holes.

I: For hitch, cut two 10 x 10 holes.

J: For pull handle pieces and lining, cut two from clear and one from white according to graph.

K: For handle joint, cut two according to graph.

STITCHING INSTRUCTIONS:

NOTE: Lining and bottom pieces are unworked.

1: For tote, using Red and Royal and stitches indicated, work one A in each color according to Tote Stitch Pattern Guide. Using Christmas Green and Yellow, work two B pieces in each color as above. Using Yellow and Christmas Green and Slanted Gobelin over narrow width, work one D piece in each color. Using colors and stitches indicated, work E pieces according to graphs. Fill in uncoded areas of puppy using White and Continental Stitch. With Black, Overcast unfinished edges of puppy and butterfly.

NOTE: Use Black for all Whip-stitching.

2: For each handle, holding one lining piece to wrong side of matching worked pieces, Whip-stitch long edges of two D pieces together. Working through all thicknesses, Whipstitch A, B and unworked C (use white piece on inside) pieces together according to Tote Assembly Diagram. Inserting ends of handles between sides and linings (see diagram) and working through all thicknesses to attach handles as you work, Whipstitch unfinished top edges of tote together.

3: For base, using Black and Slanted Gobelin Stitch over 3 bars, work two F and two G pieces according to Base Side Cutting & Stitch Pattern Guide. With Black, Overcast unfinished cutout edges of worked F pieces.

4: Holding clear J pieces together and working through both thicknesses, using Black and Alternating Slanted Gobelin Stitch, work according to graph. Fill in uncoded areas and work one I and one K using Black and Continental Stitch. With Black, sew socket half of one snap to center of unworked I. Holding I pieces wrong sides together, Whipstitch together on three sides (unfinished edge will attach to base), forming hitch.

5: Holding unworked lining pieces to wrong side of matching worked pieces, Whipstitch J and K pieces together as indicated on graphs. Whipstitch J, K and one worked G piece together as indicated and according to Pull

ach car on this fun-time train is really a separate tote bag for carrying all your little one's favorite belongings. When playtime's over, it's "All aboard!" for easy storage.

Photographed at *Satterwhite Log Homes*, Longview, Texas.

BY TRUDY BATH SMITH

TOT'S TOTE TRAIN

Handle Assembly Diagram.

6: With snap facing down, Whipstitch unfinished edge of hitch to remaining worked G according to Base Assembly Diagram. Omitting corner edges, Whipstitch unworked F and G pieces to unworked H according to Base Side Cutting & Stitch Pattern Guide and Base Assembly Diagram. Holding matching worked pieces and lining pieces wrong sides together, Whipstitch F and G pieces together. (**NOTE:** Do not Whipstitch axle cutouts together.) Whipstitch unfinished top edges of base together.

NOTE: Cut two 12" lengths of dowel.

7: For axles, insert dowels through base cutouts, glue wheels to ends of dowels. Glue motifs to tote as shown in photo. Place tote in base.

MEDIUM TOTE

CUTTING INSTRUCTIONS:

NOTE: Use white canvas for tote lining pieces.

A: For tote sides and side linings, cut two from each color 55 x 67 holes.

B: For tote end pieces and end lining pieces, cut four from each color 23 x 55 holes.

C: For tote bottom and bottom lining, cut one from each color 46 x 67 holes.

D: For handles and handles linings, cut two from each color 5 x 70 holes.

E: For medium puppy and butterfly motifs, cut one each according to graphs.

F: For base sides, cut four 10 x 69 holes; cut out axle opening at each end of each piece according to Base Side Cutting & Stitch Pattern Guide.

G: For base ends, cut four 10 x 48 holes.

H: For base bottom, cut one 48 x 69 holes.

I: For hitches, cut four 10 x 10 holes.

STITCHING INSTRUCTIONS:

1: Working sides in Royal and Yellow and end pieces and handles in Christmas Green and Red, follow Steps 1-3 of Large Tote on page 64.

2: Using Black and Continental Stitch, work two I pieces. Sew ball

half of one snap to center of one worked I. Sew socket half of one snap to center of one unworked I. For each hitch, holding one unworked I to wrong side of one worked piece, Whipstitch together on three sides.

3: Whipstitching unfinished edges of one hitch to each worked G (with ball side of snap facing up and socket side of snap facing down) and cutting 9¼" lengths of dowel, follow Steps 6-7 of Large Tote.

SMALL TOTE

CUTTING INSTRUCTIONS:

NOTE: Use white canvas for tote lining pieces.

A: For tote sides and side linings, cut two from each color 40 x 50 holes.

B: For tote end pieces and end lining pieces, cut four from each color 14 x 40 holes.

C: For tote bottom and bottom lining, cut one from each color 28 x 50 holes.

D: For handles and handles linings, cut two from each color 5 x 70 holes.

BASE SIDE CUTTING & STITCH PATTERN GUIDE

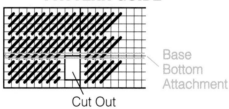

Base Bottom Attachment

Cut Out

TOTE ASSEMBLY DIAGRAM

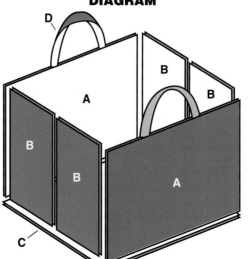

E: For butterfly motif, cut one according to Medium Butterfly E Graph.

F: For base sides, cut four 10 x 52 holes; cut out axle opening at each end of each piece according to Base Side Cutting & Stitch Pattern Guide.

G: For base ends, cut four 10 x 30 holes.

H: For base bottom, cut one 30 x 52 holes.

I: For hitch, cut two 10 x 10 holes.

STITCHING INSTRUCTIONS:

1: Working sides in Red and Christmas Green, end pieces and handles in Royal and Yellow, and substituting Yellow for Royal on butterfly, follow Steps 1-3 of Large Tote on page 64.

2: Using Black and Continental Stitch, work one I. Sew ball half of remaining snap to center of worked piece. Holding I pieces wrong sides together, Whipstitch together on three sides, forming hitch.

3: Whipstitching unfinished edges of hitch to one worked G and cutting 6½" lengths of dowel, follow Steps 6-7 of Large Tote on page 64. ✳

K – HANDLE JOINT
(cut 2)
12 x 23 holes

Do not Whipstitch; attach to pull handle.

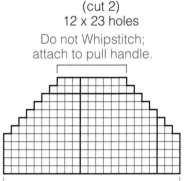

Do not Whipstitch; attach to base end.

TOTE STITCH PATTERN GUIDE

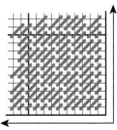

Continue established pattern up and across each entire piece.

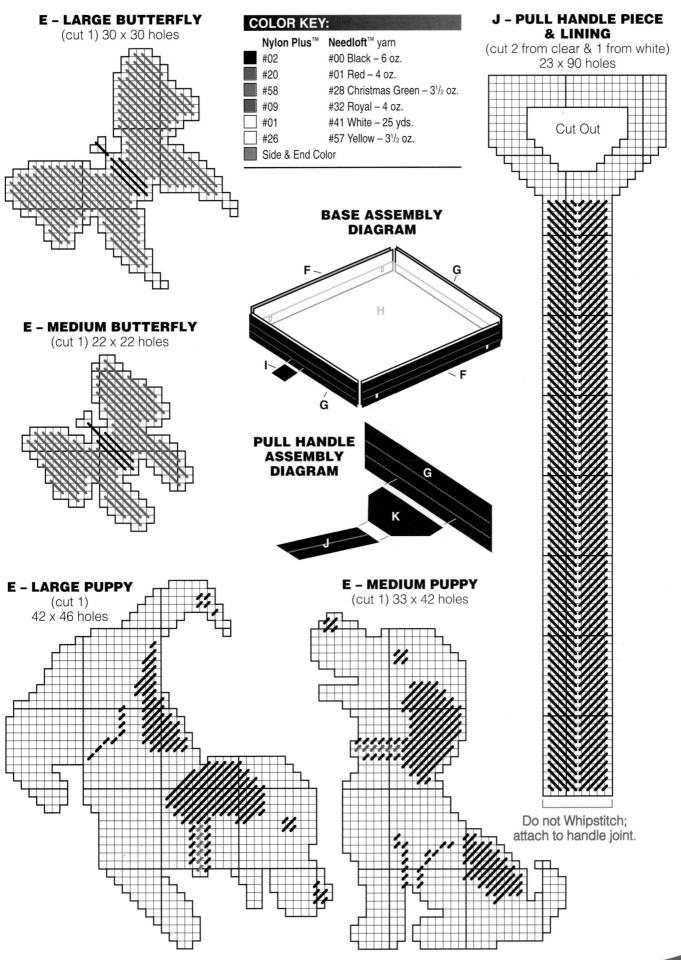

E – LARGE BUTTERFLY
(cut 1) 30 x 30 holes

E – MEDIUM BUTTERFLY
(cut 1) 22 x 22 holes

E – LARGE PUPPY
(cut 1)
42 x 46 holes

E – MEDIUM PUPPY
(cut 1) 33 x 42 holes

COLOR KEY:

Nylon Plus™	Needloft™ yarn
■ #02	#00 Black – 6 oz.
▨ #20	#01 Red – 4 oz.
▨ #58	#28 Christmas Green – 3½ oz.
▨ #09	#32 Royal – 4 oz.
□ #01	#41 White – 25 yds.
□ #26	#57 Yellow – 3½ oz.
▨ Side & End Color	

BASE ASSEMBLY DIAGRAM

PULL HANDLE ASSEMBLY DIAGRAM

J – PULL HANDLE PIECE & LINING
(cut 2 from clear & 1 from white)
23 x 90 holes

Cut Out

Do not Whipstitch;
attach to handle joint.

LADYBUG COZY

BY MICHELE WILCOX

SIZE: 6" square x 4¾" tall.

SKILL LEVEL: Easy

MATERIALS: 1½ sheets of 7-count plastic canvas; Worsted-weight or plastic canvas yarn (for amounts see Color Key).

CUTTING INSTRUCTIONS:

A: For sides, cut four according to graph.

B: For bottom, cut one 39 x 39 holes.

STITCHING INSTRUCTIONS:

1: Using colors indicated and Continental Stitch, work A pieces according to graph. Fill in uncoded areas and work B using White and Continental Stitch. Using Black for ladybugs, Christmas Green for stems, Backstitch and Straight Stitch, embroider as indicated on graphs.

2: With matching colors as shown in photo, Overcast unfinished cutout edges of A pieces. With right side of bottom facing in, with White, Whipstitch A and B pieces together; Overcast unfinished top edges.✳

Bright ladybugs and fresh daisies dress up a summertime plant cozy that's easy and fun to stitch. Cutouts around the ladybugs add peek-a-boo interest to this design, which can be used to hold a potted plant or freshly cut flowers.

A – SIDE (cut 4) 31 x 39 holes

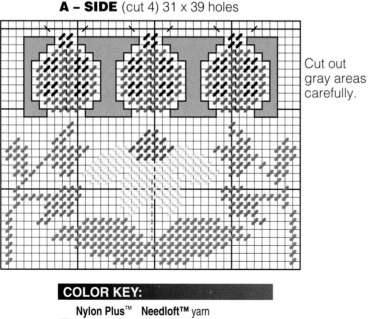

Cut out gray areas carefully.

A three-dimensional house, white picket fence and perky plaid bow set the scene for welcoming friends with this country-style door hanging.

BY NIKI RUSSOS-ATKINSON

WELCOME
DOOR HANGING

SIZE: 11¼" x 22½".

SKILL LEVEL: Easy

MATERIALS: Two sheets of 13½" x 22½" 7-count plastic canvas; 1 yd. of 3" plaid ribbon; Six-strand embroidery floss (for amount see Color Key); Worsted-weight or plastic canvas yarn (for amounts see Color Key).

CUTTING INSTRUCTIONS:

(See graphs on pages 71-73.)

A: For background, cut two according to graph.

B: For house front, cut one 23 x 35 holes.

C: For house sides, cut two according to graph.

D: For house roof, cut one 9 x 35 holes.

E: For house bottom, cut one 6 x 35 holes.

STITCHING INSTRUCTIONS:

1: Using colors indicated and Continental Stitch, work one A and B pieces according to graphs. Fill in uncoded areas on A (leaving indicated area unworked) using Sail Blue and B using White and Continental Stitch. Using Black for roof, White for sides and bottom and Continental Stitch, work C (one on opposite side of canvas), D and E pieces. Using six strands floss and Backstitch for windows and door and White and French Knot for doorknob, embroider B as indicated on graph.

2: With White, Whipstitch B, C

and E pieces together according to House Assembly Diagram; with Black, Whipstitch D to assembly. With matching colors, Whipstitch house to worked A at unworked area. Holding unworked A to wrong side of worked piece, with matching colors, Whipstitch together.

NOTE: Cut one 7" length of Sail Blue.

3: For hanger, thread each end of 7" strand through wrong side as indicated. Knot and trim ends. Tie ribbon into a two-loop bow and trim ends as shown in photo. Tack bow to bottom of door hanging.✳

COLOR KEY:

Embroidery floss		
■	Black – 4 yds.	

Nylon Plus™	**Needloft**™ yarn	
■ #02	#00 Black – 24 yds.	
▨ #20	#01 Red – 2 yds.	
▨ #44	#14 Cinnamon – 2½ yds.	
▨ #42	#21 Baby Yellow – 4 yds.	
▨ #31	#27 Holly – 10 yds.	
■ #32	#29 Forest – 4 yds.	
□ #04	#35 Sail Blue – 90 yds.	
▨ #01	#41 White – 26 yds.	
▨ #37	#53 Mermaid Green – 60 yds.	

STITCH KEY:

—	Backstitch/Straight Stitch
□	Unworked Area/House Attachment
✦	Hanger Attachment

B – HOUSE FRONT

(cut 1)

23 x 35 holes

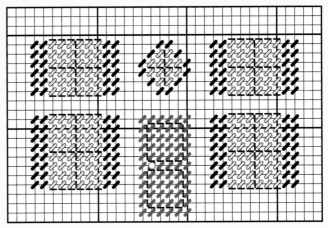

WATERMELON BASKETS
BY MICHELE WILCOX

SIZE: Large Basket is 3⅝" x 7¾" x about 9½" tall; Medium Basket is 2¾" x 5⅞" x about 7" tall; Small Basket is 1⅞" x 3⅞" x about 4½" tall.

SKILL LEVEL: Easy

MATERIALS FOR ONE: One sheet of 5-, 7- or 10-count plastic canvas (**NOTE:** Use 5-count for Large, 7-count for Medium or 10-count for Small Basket); Craft glue or glue gun; Worsted-weight or plastic canvas yarn or #3 pearl cotton or six-strand embroidery floss (for type and amounts see Color Key).

CUTTING INSTRUCTIONS:

A: For sides, cut two according to graph.

B: For ends and bottom, cut one 17 x 75 holes.

C: For handle, cut one 4 x 64 holes.

STITCHING INSTRUCTIONS:

NOTE: Use a doubled strand of worsted-weight or plastic canvas yarn for Large Basket, a single strand of worsted-weight or plastic canvas yarn for Medium Basket or a single strand of #3 pearl cotton or 12 strands floss for Small Basket.

1: Using colors and stitches indicated, work A and B pieces according to graphs. Fill in uncoded areas of A using Watermelon or Dk. Pink and Continental Stitch. Using one strand Black and French Knot (wrap around needle once or twice as desired), embroider seeds as indicated on graph. Using Forest for large, Moss for medium or Lt. Green for small basket and Scotch Stitch over 3 bars, work C; Overcast unfinished edges of handle.

2: With Forest or Dk. Green and easing to fit, Whipstitch A and B pieces together as indicated. With matching colors, Overcast unfinished top edges. Glue ends of handle inside basket as indicated.✳

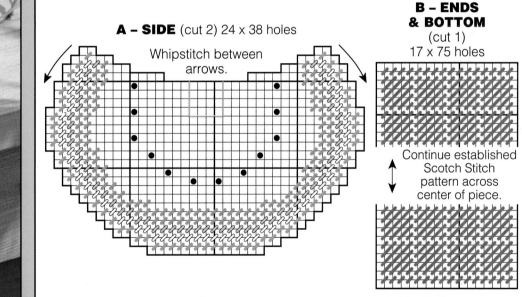

A – SIDE (cut 2) 24 x 38 holes

Whipstitch between arrows.

B – ENDS & BOTTOM
(cut 1)
17 x 75 holes

Continue established Scotch Stitch pattern across center of piece.

COLOR KEY:		Large:	Medium:	Small:
Nylon Plus™	**Needloft™ yarn**			**#3 pearl cotton or floss**
■ #02	#00 Black	6 yds.	3 yds.	Black – 3 yds.
▨ #11	#07 Pink	14 yds.	7 yds.	Pink – 7 yds.
◪ #10	#08 Baby Pink	10 yds.	5 yds.	Lt. Pink – 5 yds.
▨ #48	#25 Moss	10 yds.	11 yds.	Lt. Green – 11 yds.
▨ #32	#29 Forest	80 yds.	25 yds.	Dk. Green – 17 yds.
◪ #01	#41 White	10 yds.	5 yds.	White – 5 yds.
▢ #54	#55 Watermelon	20 yds.	16 yds.	Dk. Pink – 13 yds.

STITCH KEY:

● French Knot

— Handle Placement

Use the same graph and three different sizes of canvas to make these luscious baskets. They'll add a burst of color to your picnics and barbecues — or use them all year long to hold candy, fruit or flowers.

SIZE: Rocker is 2¾" x 5⅛" x 5⅞" tall; Dresser is 2⅛" x 5⅛" x 5⅛" tall; Crib is 3" x 5⅛" x 4⅝" tall; High Chair is 2⅛" x 2½" x 5¾" tall.

SKILL LEVEL: Average

MATERIALS FOR SET: 3½ sheets of 7-count plastic canvas; 1⅓ sheets of pink 7-count plastic canvas; Six brass paper fasteners; Worsted-weight or plastic canvas yarn (for amounts see Color Key).

ROCKER

CUTTING INSTRUCTIONS:

NOTE: Use pink canvas throughout.

A: For front and back, cut one each according to graphs.

B: For sides, cut two according to graph.

C: For seat, cut one 17 x 17 holes.

STITCHING INSTRUCTIONS:

1: Using colors and stitches indicated (work Pink Cross Stitches over Rose Long Stitches), work A and B (one on opposite side of canvas) pieces according to graphs, leaving indicated and uncoded areas unworked. With Pink, Overcast unfinished cutout edges.

2: With Pink, Whipstitch A, B and unworked C pieces together as indicated and according to Rocker Assembly Diagram. With Rose for back and arm edges and with Pink, Overcast unfinished edges.

DRESSER

CUTTING INSTRUCTIONS:

(See graphs on page 78.)

NOTE: Use clear canvas throughout.

A: For front and back, cut one according to graph and one 33 x 33 holes.

B: For sides, cut two 13 x 33 holes.

C: For top, cut one 13 x 33 holes.

D: For supports, cut three 13 x 33 holes.

E: For long drawer fronts, cut two 9 x 29 holes.

F: For long drawer backs, cut two 7 x 27 holes.

G: For long drawer sides, cut four 7 x 13 holes.

H: For long drawer bottoms, cut two 13 x 27 holes.

I: For short drawer fronts, cut two 7 x 13 holes.

J: For short drawer backs, cut two 5 x 11 holes.

K: For short drawer sides, cut four 5 x 13 holes.

L: For short drawer bottoms, cut two 11 x 13 holes.

A – ROCKER FRONT
(cut 1)
10 x 17 holes

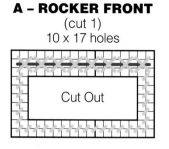

B – ROCKER SIDE
(cut 2)
26 x 33 holes

Whipstitch to front.

Whipstitch to back.

Cut Out

Cut Out

A – ROCKER BACK
(cut 1)
17 x 28 holes

Whipstitch to side.

Whipstitch to side.

Cut Out

ROCKER ASSEMBLY DIAGRAM

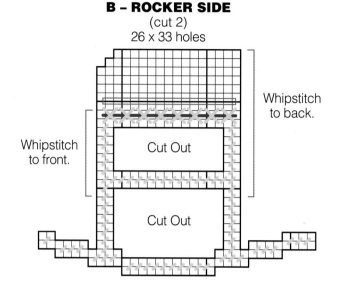

BACK A

B

C

FRONT A

B

COLOR KEY:

	Nylon Plus™	Needloft™ yarn
■	#02	#00 Black – small amount
■	#52	#06 Rose – 12 yds.
▨	#11	#07 Pink – 2 oz.
▨	#25	#20 Lemon – 1½ yds.
▨	#17	#58 Bright Orange – small amount

STITCH KEY:

— Backstitch/Straight Stitch

● French Knot

☐ Unworked Area/Support Attachment

☐ Unworked Area/Inner Drawer Attachment

☐ Bottom Attachment

☐ Unworked Area/Seat Attachment

☐ Tray Attachment

○ Brass Fastener Attachment

FASHION DOLL
NURSERY

BY OLIVE SEVERA

She'll have hours of fun with this adorable four-piece nursery set including dresser, crib, rocker and high chair.

Barbie® doll photographed by permission of Mattel, Inc.

FUNNY FRIENDS

BY SANDRA MILLER-MAXFIELD

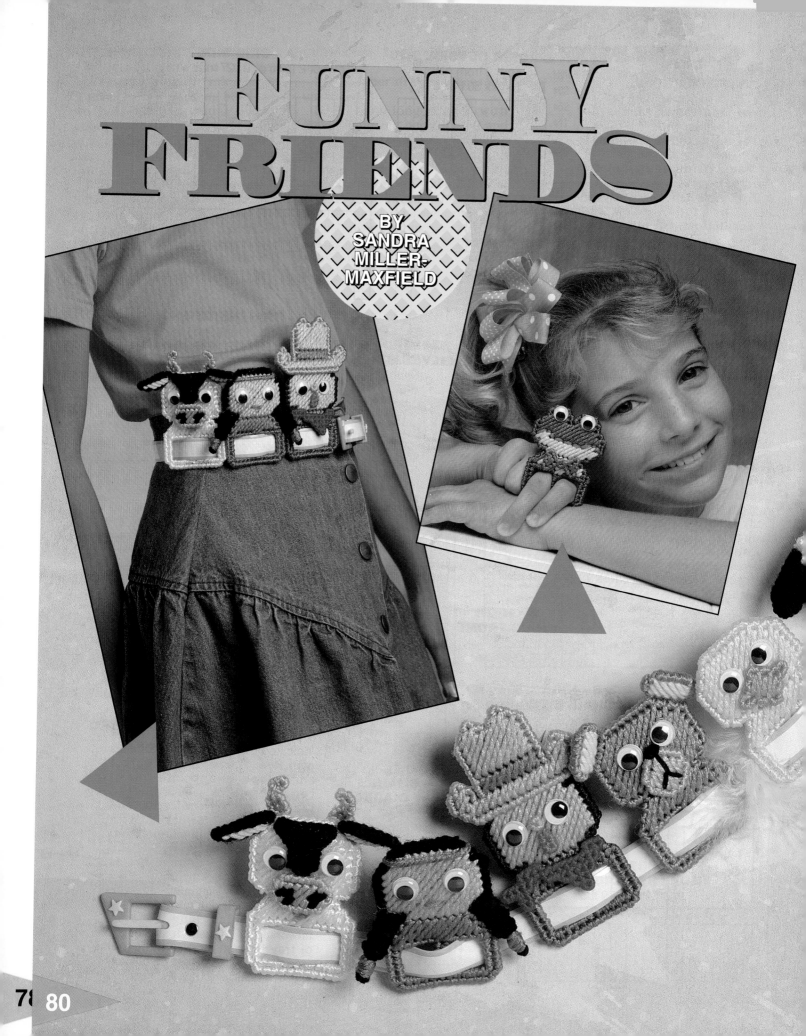

These cute critters and funny folks tag along on your belt, watchband, T-shirt or shoes. And they're finger puppets, too!

SIZE: Each is about 4" x 4½".
SKILL LEVEL: Average
MATERIALS FOR ONE: Scraps of 7-count plastic canvas; Scrap of dusty rose 7-count canvas (Granny); Two 12-mm. wiggle eyes; Three small artificial yellow feathers (Chick); One white ½" pom-pom (Bunny); Craft glue or glue gun; Worsted-weight or plastic canvas yarn (for amounts see individual Color Keys on pages 82-85).

81

BEAR

CUTTING INSTRUCTIONS:

A: For body, cut two according to graph.

B: For ears, cut four according to graph.

C: For muzzle, cut one according to graph.

STITCHING INSTRUCTIONS:

1: Using colors indicated and Slanted Gobelin Stitch, work A, two B and C pieces according to graphs. Substituting Camel for Pink, work remaining B pieces according to graph. Using Black and Straight Stitch, embroider mouth lines as indicated on C graph; with Black for nose area as shown in photo and with Tan, Overcast unfinished edges of C.

2: Holding A pieces wrong sides together, with Camel, Whipstitch together. For each ear, holding one of each color wrong sides together, with Camel, Whipstitch two B pieces together.

3: Glue ears, muzzle and eyes to body as shown.

BUNNY

CUTTING INSTRUCTIONS:

A: For body, cut two according to Bear A Graph.

B: For ears, cut four according to graph.

C: For muzzle, cut one according to graph.

D: For nose, cut one according to graph.

STITCHING INSTRUCTIONS:

1: Using colors indicated and Slanted Gobelin Stitch, work A, two B (one on opposite side of canvas) and C pieces according to graphs. Substituting Tan for Pink, work remaining B pieces (one on opposite side of canvas) according to graph. With Watermelon for nose and with White for muzzle, Overcast unfinished edges of C and D pieces.

2: With Tan for body and ears, follow Step 2 of Bear.

3: Glue nose to muzzle and muzzle, ears and eyes to body as shown in photo.

CHICK

CUTTING INSTRUCTIONS:

A: For body, cut two according to Bear A Graph.

B: For beak, cut one according to graph.

STITCHING INSTRUCTIONS:

1: Using colors indicated and Slanted Gobelin Stitch, work A and B pieces according to graphs. With Tangerine, Overcast unfinished edges of B.

2: Holding A pieces wrong sides together, with Straw, Whipstitch together. Glue beak, eyes and feathers to body as shown in photo.

CHICK COLOR KEY:

Nylon Plus™	Needloft™ yarn
#15	#11 Tangerine – 1 yd.
#41	#19 Straw – 6 yds.

B – CHICK BEAK
(cut 1)
5 x 7 holes

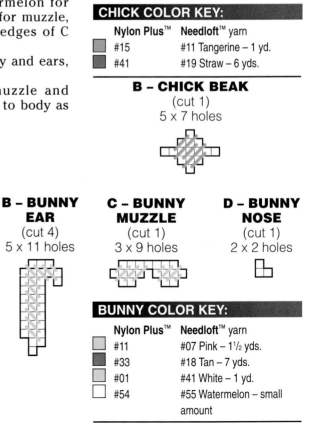

B – BEAR EAR
(cut 4)
4 x 6 holes

C – BEAR MUZZLE
(cut 1)
5 x 5 holes
Top

A – BEAR BODY
(cut 2)
13 x 19 holes

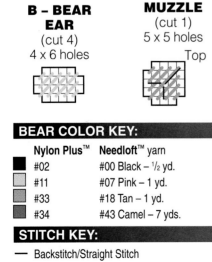

Cut Out   Cut Out

B – BUNNY EAR
(cut 4)
5 x 11 holes

C – BUNNY MUZZLE
(cut 1)
3 x 9 holes

D – BUNNY NOSE
(cut 1)
2 x 2 holes

BEAR COLOR KEY:

Nylon Plus™	Needloft™ yarn
#02	#00 Black – ½ yd.
#11	#07 Pink – 1 yd.
#33	#18 Tan – 1 yd.
#34	#43 Camel – 7 yds.

STITCH KEY:

— Backstitch/Straight Stitch

BUNNY COLOR KEY:

Nylon Plus™	Needloft™ yarn
#11	#07 Pink – 1½ yds.
#33	#18 Tan – 7 yds.
#01	#41 White – 1 yd.
#54	#55 Watermelon – small amount

COW

CUTTING INSTRUCTIONS:

A: For body, cut two according to Bear A Graph.

B: For ears, cut four according to graph.

C: For patch, cut one according to graph.

D: For muzzle, cut one according to graph.

E: For horns, cut two according to graph.

STITCHING INSTRUCTIONS:

1: Using colors indicated and Slanted Gobelin Stitch, work A, two B (one on opposite side of canvas), C, D and E (one on opposite side of canvas) pieces according to graphs. Substituting Black for Pink, work remaining B pieces (one on opposite side of canvas). With Flesh Tone for muzzle and with matching colors, Overcast unfinished edges of C-E pieces.

2: With White for body and Black for ears, follow Step 2 of Bear on page 82.

3: For tongue, glue a small loop of Watermelon to bottom of muzzle as shown in photo. Glue horns, muzzle, patch, ears and eyes to body as shown.

COWBOY

CUTTING INSTRUCTIONS:

A: For body, cut two according to graph.

B: For hat, cut two according to graph.

C: For scarf, cut one according to graph.

D: For mouth, cut one 1 x 2 holes.

E: For nose, cut one 1 x 1 hole.

STITCHING INSTRUCTIONS:

1: Using colors indicated and Slanted Gobelin Stitch, work one A, B and C pieces according to graphs. For back A, substituting Brown for Flesh Tone, work remaining A piece according to graph. With Flesh Tone for nose, Watermelon for mouth and Red for scarf, Overcast unfinished edges of C-E pieces.

2: Holding A pieces wrong sides together, with Brown for head and with Turquoise, Whipstitch together. For hat, holding B pieces wrong sides together, with Tan,

Whipstitch together as indicated on graph; Overcast unfinished edges.

3: Glue hat, nose, mouth, eyes and scarf to body as shown in photo.

COWBOY COLOR KEY:

	Nylon Plus™	Needloft™ yarn
	#20	#01 Red – 2 yds.
	#35	#13 Maple – ½ yd.
	#36	#15 Brown – 2 yds.
	#33	#18 Tan – 4 yds.
	#03	#54 Turquoise – 2½ yds.
	#54	#55 Watermelon – small amount
	#14	#56 Flesh Tone – 2 yds.

A – COWBOY BODY
(cut 2)
13 x 19 holes

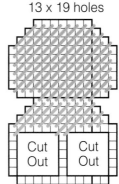

B – COWBOY HAT
(cut 2)
11 x 17 holes

Whipstitch between arrows.

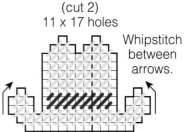

C – COWBOY SCARF
(cut 1)
5 x 14 holes

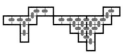

D – COWBOY MOUTH
(cut 1)
1 x 2 holes

B – COW EAR
(cut 4)
3 x 7 holes

C – COW PATCH
(cut 1)
6 x 7 holes

D – COW MUZZLE
(cut 1)
4 x 7 holes

E – COW HORN
(cut 2)
4 x 4 holes

COW COLOR KEY:

	Nylon Plus™	Needloft™ yarn
	#02	#00 Black – 2 yds.
	#11	#07 Pink – ½ yd.
	#33	#18 Tan – 1 yd.
	#01	#41 White – 7 yds.
	#14	#56 Flesh Tone – 1 yd.
	#54	#55 Watermelon – small amount

ELEPHANT

CUTTING INSTRUCTIONS:

A: For body, cut two according to Bear A Graph on page 82.

B: For ears, cut four according to graph.

C: For trunk, cut two according to graph.

STITCHING INSTRUCTIONS:

1: Using colors indicated and Slanted Gobelin Stitch, work A, two B (one on opposite side on canvas) and C (one on opposite side of canvas) pieces according to graphs. Substituting Gray for Pink, work remaining B pieces (one on opposite side of canvas) according to graph.

2: With Gray, follow Step 2 of Bear on page 82. Holding C pieces wrong sides together, Whipstitch together.

3: Glue ears, trunk and eyes to body as shown in photo.

FROG

CUTTING INSTRUCTIONS:

A: For body, cut two according to graph.

B: For bow tie, cut one according to graph.

STITCHING INSTRUCTIONS:

1: Using colors indicated and Slanted Gobelin Stitch, work one A and B piece according to graphs. For back A, using Holly and Slanted Gobelin Stitch, work remaining A piece according to Bear A Graph. Using Watermelon and Backstitch, embroider mouth on front as indicated on graph. With Turquoise, Overcast unfinished edges of B.

2: Holding A pieces wrong sides together, with Holly, Whipstitch together. Glue bow tie and eyes to body as shown in photo.

INDIAN GIRL

CUTTING INSTRUCTIONS:

A: For body, cut two according to Cowboy A Graph on page 83.

B: For braids, cut two according to graph.

STITCHING INSTRUCTIONS:

1: Using colors and stitches indicated, work one A and B pieces according to graphs. For back A, substituting Black for Flesh Tone, work remaining A piece according to graph. Using Watermelon and a single Straight Stitch over 2 bars, embroider mouth on front A as shown in photo. With Black, Overcast unfinished edges of C pieces.

2: Holding A pieces wrong sides together, with Black for head and with Maple, Whipstitch together.

NOTE: Cut one 5" and two 3" lengths each of Turquoise and Watermelon.

3: For headband, twist 5" lengths of Turquoise and Watermelon together and tie around head as shown; knot and trim ends. For each braid, holding one 3" length each of Turquoise and Watermelon

B – ELEPHANT EAR
(cut 4)
9 x 9 holes

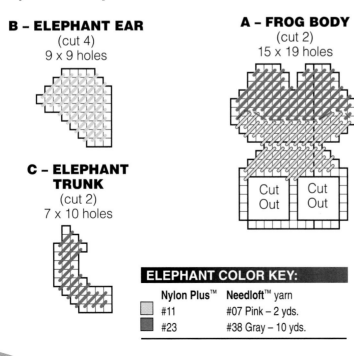

C – ELEPHANT TRUNK
(cut 2)
7 x 10 holes

A – FROG BODY
(cut 2)
15 x 19 holes

Cut Out   Cut Out

B – FROG BOW TIE
(cut 1)
7 x 7 holes

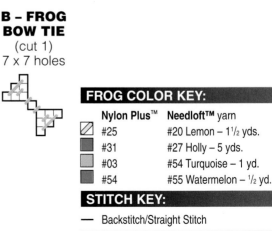

ELEPHANT COLOR KEY:

	Nylon Plus™	Needloft™ yarn
	#11	#07 Pink – 2 yds.
	#23	#38 Gray – 10 yds.

FROG COLOR KEY:

	Nylon Plus™	Needloft™ yarn
⧄	#25	#20 Lemon – 1½ yds.
	#31	#27 Holly – 5 yds.
	#03	#54 Turquoise – 1 yd.
	#54	#55 Watermelon – ½ yd.

STITCH KEY:

— Backstitch/Straight Stitch

together, wrap tightly around narrow end of one B as shown; glue ends to secure. Glue braids and eyes to body as shown in photo.

B – INDIAN GIRL BRAID
(cut 2)
8 x 8 holes

INDIAN GIRL COLOR KEY:

Nylon Plus™	Needloft™ yarn
#02	#00 Black – 3½ yds.
#35	#13 Maple – 3 yds.
#03	#54 Turquoise – small amount
#54	#55 Watermelon – small amount
#14	#56 Flesh Tone – 2 yds.

GRANNY COLOR KEY:

Nylon Plus™	Needloft™ yarn
#23	#38 Gray – 3 yds.
#03	#54 Turquoise – 3 yds.
#54	#55 Watermelon – small amount
#14	#56 Flesh Tone – 2 yds.

B – GRANNY HAIR BUN
(cut 2)
4 x 6 holes

C – GRANNY EYEGLASSES
(cut 1 from dusty rose)
2 x 13 holes

Cut out gray areas carefully.

GRANNY

CUTTING INSTRUCTIONS:
NOTE: Use dusty rose canvas for eyeglasses.
A: For body, cut two according to Cowboy A Graph on page 83.
B: For hair bun, cut two according to graph.
C: For eyeglasses, cut one from dusty rose according to graph.
D: For nose, cut one 1 x 2 holes.
E: For mouth, cut one according to Bunny D Graph on page 82.

STITCHING INSTRUCTIONS:
1: Using colors indicated and Slanted Gobelin Stitch, work one A and B pieces according to graphs. Substituting Gray for Flesh Tone, work remaining A piece according to graph. With Flesh Tone for nose and Watermelon for mouth, Overcast unfinished edges of D and E pieces.
2: Holding A pieces wrong sides together, with Gray for head and with Turquoise, Whipstitch together. For bun, holding B pieces wrong sides together, with Gray, Whipstitch together. Glue bun, nose, mouth, eyes and glasses to body as shown in photo.

B – LAMB EAR
(cut 2)
4 x 7 holes

C – LAMB MUZZLE
(cut 1)
4 x 7 holes

LAMB

CUTTING INSTRUCTIONS:
A: For body, cut two according to Bear A Graph on page 82.
B: For ears, cut two according to graph.
C: For muzzle, cut one according to graph.

STITCHING INSTRUCTIONS:
1: Using White and French Knot, work one stitch in each hole on one A piece for front. For back A, using White and Slanted Gobelin Stitch, work remaining A piece according to Bear A Graph on page 82. Using Black and Slanted Gobelin Stitch, work B (one on opposite side of canvas) and C pieces according to graphs. Using Pink and Fly Stitch, embroider mouth as indicated on graph. With Pink for nose area as shown in photo and with Black, Overcast unfinished edges of B and C pieces.
2: Holding A pieces wrong sides together, with White, Whipstitch together. Glue ears, eyes and muzzle to body as shown. ✳

LAMB COLOR KEY:

Nylon Plus™	Needloft™ yarn
#02	#00 Black – 3 yds.
#11	#07 Pink – ½ yd.
#01	#41 White – 10 yds.

STITCH KEY:
✢ Fly Stitch

The Colors of Autumn

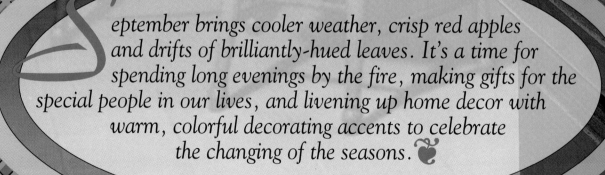

September brings cooler weather, crisp red apples and drifts of brilliantly-hued leaves. It's a time for spending long evenings by the fire, making gifts for the special people in our lives, and livening up home decor with warm, colorful decorating accents to celebrate the changing of the seasons.

Photographed at *Satterwhite Log Homes*, Longview, Texas

BY ELEANOR ALBANO

BRICK RUG

Cozy up a chilly floor with this casual area rug — it has all the warmth of an old-fashioned red brick hearth.

SIZE: 25¾" x 41¼", not including fringe.

SKILL LEVEL: Easy

MATERIALS: Nine sheets of 7-count plastic canvas; 13" square cardboard; Rug or plastic canvas yarn (for amounts see Color Key).

CUTTING INSTRUCTIONS:

A: For large blocks, cut thirty-two 24 x 54 holes.

B: For small blocks, cut six 24 x 27 holes.

STITCHING INSTRUCTIONS:

1: Using tan and Continental Stitch, work A and B pieces according to graphs. Fill in uncoded areas of each block using colors indicated on Rug Color & Assembly Diagram and Continental Stitch.

2: With tan, Whipstitch blocks together according to diagram. With tan, Overcast unfinished long edges of rug.

NOTE: For fringe, wrap tan around cardboard 20-25 times; cut strands at each end, making 13" lengths. You will need a total of 348 strands.

3: Work fringe in each hole and over last stitch of each seam on short ends of rug according to Steps 1 and 2 of Fringe Diagram. Trim ends to even.

COLOR KEY:

Rug or plastic canvas yarn

☐ Tan – 12 oz.
☐ Red – 2½ oz.
☐ Med. Brown – 2½ oz.
☐ Dk. Brown – 2 oz.
☐ Dk. Orange – 2 oz.
☐ Med. Red – 2 oz.
☐ Red-Brown – 2 oz.
☐ Rust – 2 oz.

B – SMALL BLOCK
(cut 6) 24 x 27 holes

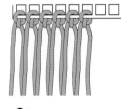

A – LARGE BLOCK
(cut 32) 24 x 54 holes

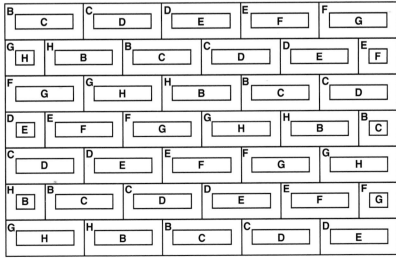

RUG COLOR & ASSEMBLY DIAGRAM

FRINGE DIAGRAM

Step 1:
Thread one 13" strand through each hole; pull ends to even and tie in square knot.

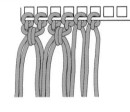

Step 2:
Tie first two knotted strands together in square knot. Repeat with next two and continue across.

KEY:

B = Dk. Brown
C = Dk. Red
D = Med. Brown
E = Red-Brown
F = Med. Red
G = Dk. Orange
H = Rust

NUMBER OF BLOCKS IN EACH COLOR COMBINATION:

B / C = 5 Large, 1 Small
C / D = 6 Large
D / E = 5 Large, 1 Small
E / F = 4 Large, 1 Small
F / G = 4 Large, 1 Small
G / H = 4 Large, 1 Small
H / B = 4 Large, 1 Small

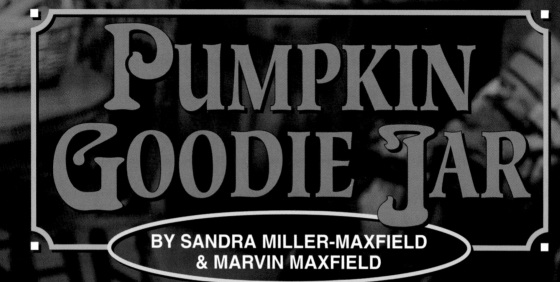

Fill this garden-fresh pumpkin with freshly baked cookies, candies or other goodies for tasty fall entertaining.

PUMPKIN GOODIE JAR

BY SANDRA MILLER-MAXFIELD & MARVIN MAXFIELD

SIZE: 7¼" across x about 10" tall.
SKILL LEVEL: Average
MATERIALS: Two sheets of 5-count plastic canvas; 1 yd. brown 1/16" bendable ribbon; 2-liter plastic beverage bottle; Polyester fiberfill; Pencil; Craft glue or glue gun; Worsted-weight or plastic canvas yarn (for amounts see Color Key).

CUTTING INSTRUCTIONS:

A: For jar side pieces, cut fifteen according to graph.

B: For lid top and jar bottom, cut one each according to graph.

C: For leaves, cut two according to graph.

D: For stem, cut two according to graph.

E: For stem top, cut one 3 x 3 holes.

F: For lid lip, cut one 4 x 66 holes.

STITCHING INSTRUCTIONS:

NOTE: Use two strands held together except for Backstitching.

1: Using colors and stitches indicated, work A, C, D (one on opposite side of canvas) and E pieces according to graphs. Using Pumpkin and Continental Stitch, work one B for lid top; Overcast unfinished edges.

2: For jar side, holding A pieces right sides together, with Pumpkin, Backstitch together at long edges as indicated on graph. Before joining last pieces, turn work right sides out, working last seam on inside. Whipstitch X edges of each A piece together as indicated. Whipstitch unworked bottom B to one end of jar side. Overcast unfinished top edges of jar.

3: With Pumpkin, Whipstitch short ends of unworked F together, forming circle; Overcast one edge. Tack unfinished edge of lip to center of wrong side on lid top.

4: For each leaf, with Mint, Whipstitch edges of each side slot on one C piece together. With right sides together, fold along center and Whipstitch X edges together as indicated; Overcast unfinished edges. Bend tip of leaf down.

5: For stem, holding D pieces wrong sides together, with Cinnamon, Whipstitch together as indicated. Squeezing seams of stem together to open, Whipstitch

E to top of stem; Overcast unfinished bottom edges.

NOTES: For jar liner, cut bottle 6½" from bottom edge. Cut bendable ribbon into four 9" lengths.

6: Place liner in jar; stuff lightly with fiberfill between liner and jar side. Stuff stem, and glue bottom to center of lid top. Fold three lengths of ribbon in half. Gluing folded end of two pieces of ribbon to wrong side of leaf near stem end, glue one leaf to lid top as shown in photo. Repeat with remaining folded and non-folded ribbon pieces and leaf. Wrap each ribbon around pencil to curl. ❧

B – LID TOP & JAR BOTTOM
(cut 1 each)
23 x 23 holes

C – LEAF
(cut 2)
26 x 27 holes

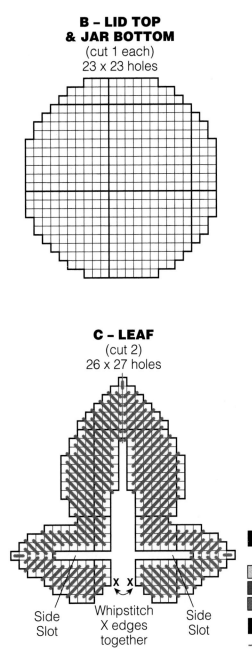

Side Slot

Whipstitch X edges together

Side Slot

A – JAR SIDE PIECE
(cut 15) 11 x 38 holes

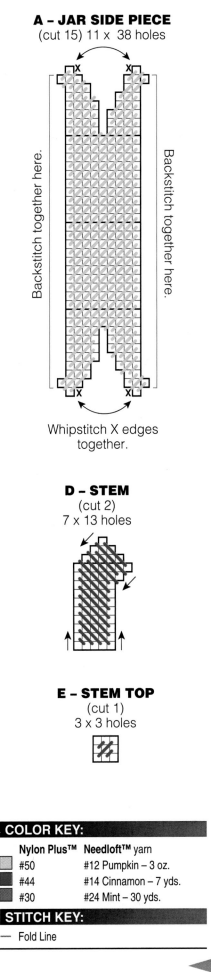

Backstitch together here.

Backstitch together here.

Whipstitch X edges together.

D – STEM
(cut 2)
7 x 13 holes

E – STEM TOP
(cut 1)
3 x 3 holes

COLOR KEY:		
Nylon Plus™	**Needloft™ yarn**	
#50	#12 Pumpkin – 3 oz.	
#44	#14 Cinnamon – 7 yds.	
#30	#24 Mint – 30 yds.	

STITCH KEY:	
— Fold Line	

91

FANCIFUL FELINES

BY TRUDY BATH SMITH

f you love quilts and cats, this magazine holder and matching tissue cover were created just for you. The easy-to-stitch quilt motifs can be made in any color combination to blend with your decor.

B – HOLDER END & END LINING
(cut 4 from clear & 2 from black)
31 x 89 holes

Cut Out

SIZE: Holder is 5" x 13¼" x 13½" tall; Tissue Cover snugly covers a boutique-style tissue box.

SKILL LEVEL: Average

MATERIALS: Five sheets of 7-count plastic canvas; Four sheets of black 7-count plastic canvas; Worsted-weight or plastic canvas yarn (for amounts see Color Key).

CUTTING INSTRUCTIONS:
(See graphs on pages 93 & 94.)

NOTE: Use black canvas for holder linings and bottom.

A: For Holder sides and side linings, cut two from each color 70 x 87 holes.

B: For Holder ends and end linings, cut four from clear and two from black according to graph.

C: For Holder bottom and bottom lining, cut two from black 31 x 87 holes.

D: For Tissue Cover top, cut one according to graph.

E: For Tissue Cover sides, cut four 30 x 37 holes.

STITCHING INSTRUCTIONS:
NOTE: Leave lining and bottom pieces unworked.

1: Using colors and stitches indicated, work A, D and E pieces according to graphs. For each end, holding two clear B pieces together and working through both thicknesses, using Black and Alternating Slanted Gobelin Stitch, work

according to graph.

2: For Holder, holding one unworked lining piece to wrong side of each end, with Black, Whipstitch unfinished cutout edges together. Holding unworked A pieces to wrong side of worked pieces and holding C pieces together, Whipstitch A, B and C pieces together through all thicknesses; Whipstitch unfinished top edges together.

3: For Tissue Cover, with Black, Overcast unfinished cutout edges of D. Whipstitch D and E pieces together; Overcast unfinished edges.❧

E – TISSUE COVER SIDE
(cut 4 from clear) 30 x 37 holes

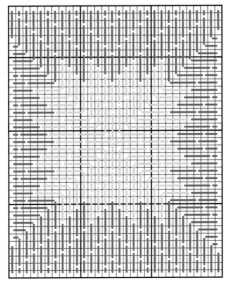

COLOR KEY:

	Nylon Plus™	Needloft™ yarn	
■	#02	#00 Black	3½ oz.
▨	#52	#06 Rose	72 yds.
▨	#01	#41 White	56 yds.
▨	#53	#42 Crimson	70 yds.

93

A – HOLDER SIDE
(cut 2 from each color) 70 x 87 holes

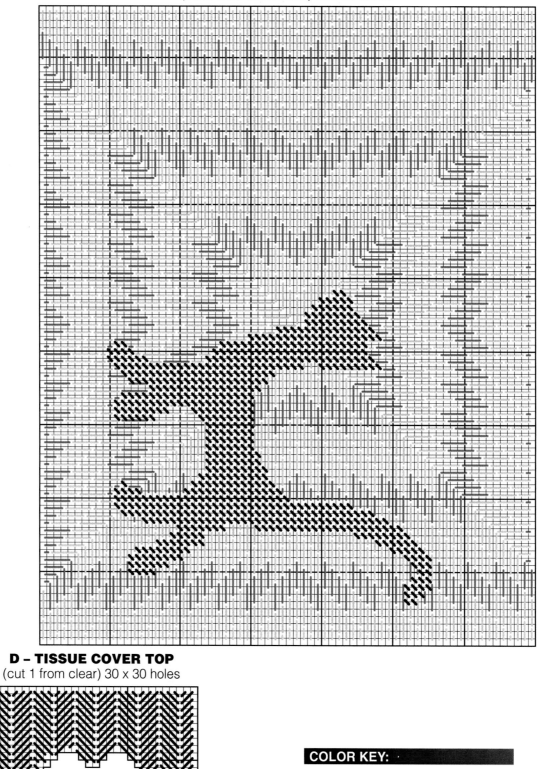

D – TISSUE COVER TOP
(cut 1 from clear) 30 x 30 holes

Cut Out

COLOR KEY:

	Nylon Plus™	Needloft™ yarn
■	#02	#00 Black – 3½ oz.
▦	#52	#06 Rose – 72 yds.
▦	#01	#41 White – 56 yds.
▦	#53	#42 Crimson – 70 yds.

APPLES
Galore

BY JOCELYN SASS

Keep track of your keys, memos, kitchen towels and even the time with this set of handy kitchen accents. Crisp as an autumn morning, these apples make especially lovely gifts for your favorite teacher.

Instructions begin on page 96

SIZE: Clock fits inside an 8" x 10" frame; Memo & Key Holder is 5½" x 13"; Towel Topper is 5" x 7⅜".

SKILL LEVEL: Easy

MATERIALS FOR SET: 1½ sheets of 7-count plastic canvas; 1½ sheets of red 7-count plastic canvas; 8" x 10" red frame with deep back; ⅜" mini clock movement; Three 1" plastic rings; Two 1" drapery hooks; 3" x 10" piece of ⅛"-thick corkboard; Kitchen towel; Sewing needle and thread to match towel; Craft glue or glue gun; Worsted-weight or plastic canvas yarn (for amounts see Color Key).

CUTTING INSTRUCTIONS:

A: For Clock, cut one from each color according to graph.

B: For Memo & Key Holder, cut one from each color according to graph.

C: For Towel Topper, cut one from each color according to graph.

STITCHING INSTRUCTIONS:

NOTE: Red canvas pieces are unworked.

1: Using colors indicated and Continental Stitch, work A, B and C pieces according to graphs. Fill in uncoded areas of A using White and B and C pieces using Red and Continental Stitch.

2: For Clock, holding unworked A to wrong side of worked piece, with Red, Whipstitch cutout edges together; do not Whipstitch outside edges together. Insert in frame; glue to hold. Attach clock movement through cutout according to manufacturer's instructions.

NOTE: Cut three 2¾" circles from corkboard.

3: For Memo & Key Holder, slip drapery hooks into B as indicated on graph. Holding unworked B to wrong side of worked piece, with matching colors, Whipstitch together. Glue cork circles to center front of each apple as shown in photo. Glue bottom edges of two plastic rings to back as indicated.

4: For Towel Topper, holding unworked C to wrong side of worked piece, with White for bottom edges as shown and with matching colors, Whipstitch together. Cut towel in half crosswise; turn cut edge ¼" to wrong side and sew hem. Run a line of gathering stitches across hemmed edge. Gather and fold sides back according to Towel Diagram; glue to bottom back of topper. Glue bottom edge of plastic ring to back (see diagram).❦

A – CLOCK
(cut 1 from each color)
53 x 67 holes

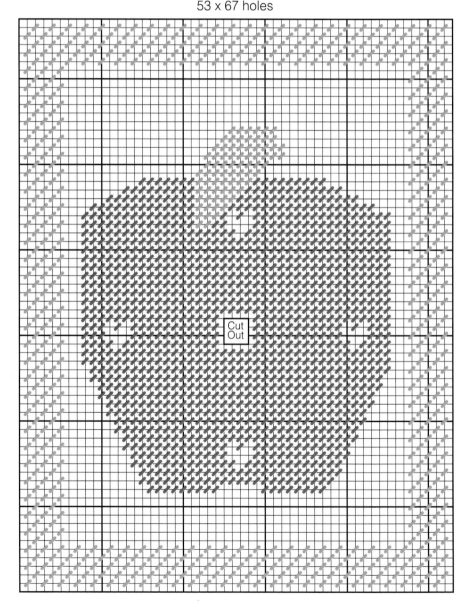

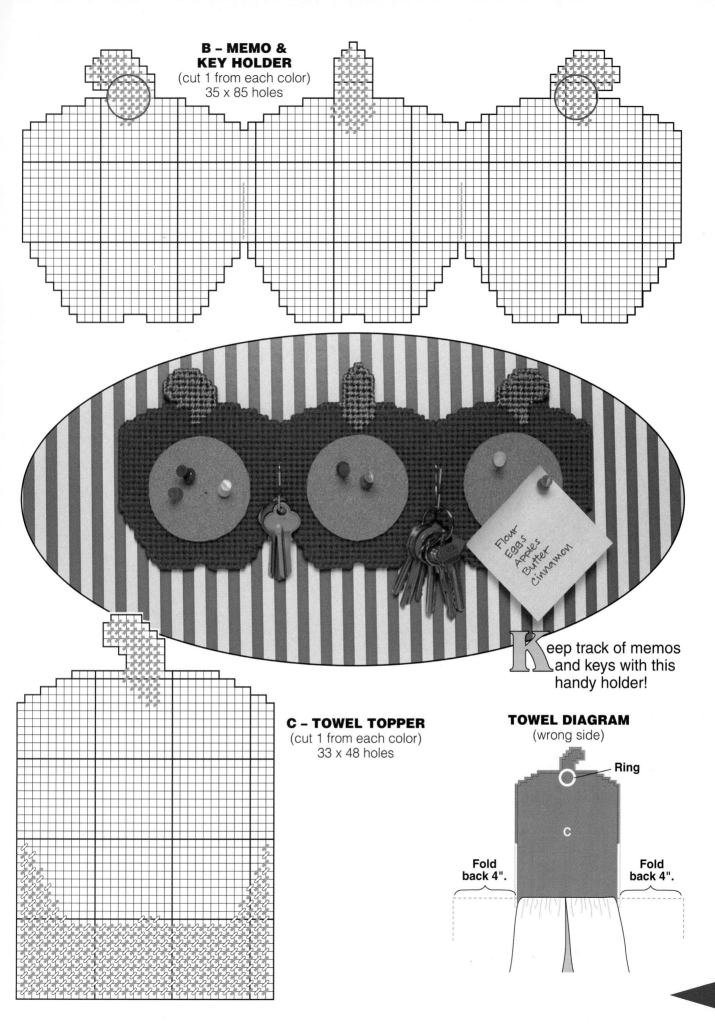

**B – MEMO &
KEY HOLDER**
(cut 1 from each color)
35 x 85 holes

C – TOWEL TOPPER
(cut 1 from each color)
33 x 48 holes

Keep track of memos
and keys with this
handy holder!

TOWEL DIAGRAM
(wrong side)

Ring

Fold
back 4".

Fold
back 4".

Flour
Eggs
Apples
Butter
Cinnamon

97

FRIENDLY
SCARECROW
BY TRUDY BATH SMITH

SIZE: 14" tall.

SKILL LEVEL: Challenging

MATERIALS: Four sheets of 7-count plastic canvas; One sheet of beige 7-count plastic canvas; 4" x 12" scrap of orange gingham fabric; Scraps of calico fabric; 22 yds. natural raffia straw; 1 yd. jute cord (optional); Green 12" x 3-mm. chenille stem; Round toothpick; Pencil; Craft glue or glue gun; Worsted-weight or plastic canvas yarn (for amounts see Color Key on page 101).

CUTTING INSTRUCTIONS:

(See graphs on pages 100-102.)

NOTE: Use beige canvas for rake pieces and rake divider.

A: For head front and back, cut one each according to graph.

B: For shirt front and back, cut one each according to graph.

C: For sleeves, cut two according to graph.

D: For right and left pant legs, cut one each according to graphs.

E: For hat top, cut one according to graph.

F: For hat brim, cut one according to graph.

G: For fence posts, cut four according to graph.

H: For fence rails, cut four 5 x 64 holes.

I: For base, cut two according to graph.

J: For tall and short pumpkins, cut two each according to graphs.

K: For pumpkin stems, cut four 2 x 3 holes.

L: For crows, cut ten according to graph.

M: For rake pieces, cut five from beige according to graph.

N: For rake divider, cut one from beige according to graph, carefully cutting through bars at red lines as indicated.

O: For scarf, fold and cut gingham fabric according to Scarf Cutting Diagram on page 102.

STITCHING INSTRUCTIONS:

1: Using colors and stitches indicated, work A-D (omit overlap area stitches on pants legs), F, G, one I, J and L (five on opposite side of canvas) pieces according to graphs. Overlapping short ends as indicated on graph and working through both thicknesses to join, using Camel and Continental Stitch, work E according to graph. Using Maple and Slanted Gobelin Stitch over narrow width, work H pieces. Using Forest and Continental Stitch, work K pieces. Using Denim and French Knot, embroider eyes on crows as indicated.

2: For head, holding edges wrong sides together, with Eggshell, Whipstitch X edges of each A piece together as indicated. Using Maple, Backstitch and Running Stitch for mouth and seam, Rust and Satin Stitch for nose, and Black and French Knot for eyes, embroider face on front A as indicated. Holding A pieces wrong sides together, with Eggshell, Whipstitch together.

3: For shirt, with Aqua, Whipstitch X edges at top of each B piece together as indicated. For each piece, folding one B along fold line wrong sides together as indicated, Whipstitch center cutout edges together. Holding B pieces wrong sides together, Whipstitch side edges together as indicated; Overcast unfinished edges.

4: For sleeves, with Aqua, Overcast edges of slot and side on each C piece as indicated. Folding each piece wrong sides together as indicated, Whipstitch unfinished side edges together as indicated; Overcast unfinished top and bottom edges.

5: For pants, with Denim, Overcast edges of slot and side on left leg D as indicated. For front and back seams, overlapping three holes at upper edge of each D piece as indicated and working through both thicknesses, work remaining stitches according to graphs. Whipstitch unfinished inseam and crotch edges together; Overcast unfinished edges.

6: For hat, with Camel, Whipstitch X edges of E together as indicated; Overcast unfinished bottom edge and outer edge of F. Glue hat top to center of brim.

NOTE: For pumpkin vines, cut chenille stem in half. Wrap each piece loosely around a pencil to curl.

7: For each pumpkin, with Bittersweet, Whipstitch X edges of each J piece together as indicated. Holding matching pieces wrong sides together, Whipstitch together. Holding two K pieces wrong sides together, with Forest, Whipstitch together. Glue one end of one vine inside center top of each pumpkin. Glue short end of one stem to top of each pumpkin over vine.

8: For each crow, holding two L pieces wrong sides together, with Tangerine for beak and with Black, Whipstitch together as indicated. With Black, Overcast unfinished edges.

9: For each fence post, holding two G pieces wrong sides together, with Maple, Whipstitch together as indicated. Whipstitch bottom edge of each post to worked I as indicated. For each rail, holding two H pieces wrong sides together, Whipstitch together. Insert rails through slots in posts. Holding unworked I to wrong side of worked piece, with Forest, Whipstitch together.

NOTE: Cut one 20" and one 12" length of Camel.

10: For rake, thread 20" strand of Camel in needle; holding unworked M pieces together, insert needle through all thicknesses ¾" from top, and pull strand through until 1" end remains. Covering 1" end, wrap strand around rake 12 times. Insert needle through all thicknesses and run end under wraps; trim excess and glue to secure. With 12" strand, beginning 3½" from bottom and wrapping six times, repeat as with 20" strand. Insert front edge of one M into each slot on N; glue to secure.

11: To shape each sleeve, allowing Overcast edges of upper section to lap over, bend lower section inward until Whipstitched edges meet; glue in place. To shape left leg, allowing lower section to lap over upper section, bend lower section inward until Whipstitched edges meet; glue in place.

NOTE: For straw, cut 21 yds. of raffia into 3"-5" lengths.

This friendly fellow may not scare the crows away, but he'll dress up an entry hall or harvest table with country charm. Complete with raffia straw stuffing, pumpkins and his own hay rake, he'll bring a crisp, autumnal air to your decor.

12: For hair, tightly tie centers of about 20 lengths of raffia together; glue lengths to top of head. Make two more bunches with about 10 lengths per bunch; glue inside front and back of neck opening on shirt as shown in photo.

13: For hands and feet, make four bunches as in Step 12 with about 25 lengths per bunch; fold in half at tie and glue one bunch inside each sleeve and pant leg opening. Using five or six lengths, make eight more bunches; set aside. For belt, wrap jute cord or one yd. of Camel yarn twice around waist and tie in square knot.

14: Positioning as shown in photo, glue head, shirt, pants and hat together. Glue small bunches of raffia inside bottom edge of shirt. Collapsing underside of right sleeve according to photo at right, glue sleeves in place as shown. Fray edges of scarf; tie around neck and glue in place as shown.

NOTE: Cut remaining raffia into ½"-1½" lengths.

15: For patches, glue one small, fray-edged scrap of fabric to each elbow and bent knee. Glue crows to scarecrow and fence rail, pumpkins to base, small raffia lengths to base and rake to scarecrow and base as shown. Wedge toothpick between inside bottom of left leg and base to stabilize scarecrow.

B – SHIRT FRONT & BACK
(cut 1 each) 27 x 33 holes

Whipstitch X edges together.

Whipstitch between arrows.

Whipstitch between arrows.

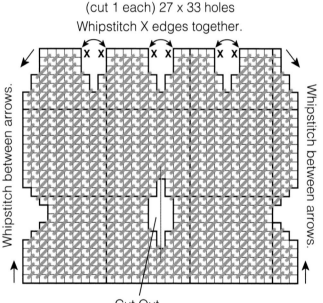

Cut Out

C – SLEEVE
(cut 2) 19 x 32 holes

Whipstitch to opposite side.

Overcast

Overcast

Whipstitch to opposite side.

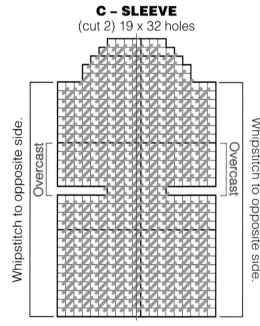

J – TALL PUMPKIN
(cut 2) 19 x 21 holes

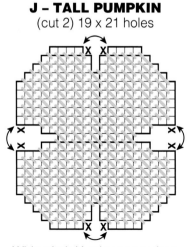

Whipstitch X edges together.

J – SHORT PUMPKIN
(cut 2) 19 x 21 holes

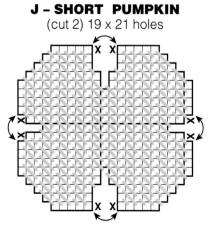

Whipstitch X edges together.

A – HEAD FRONT & BACK
(cut 1 each) 19 x 21 holes

Whipstitch X edges together.

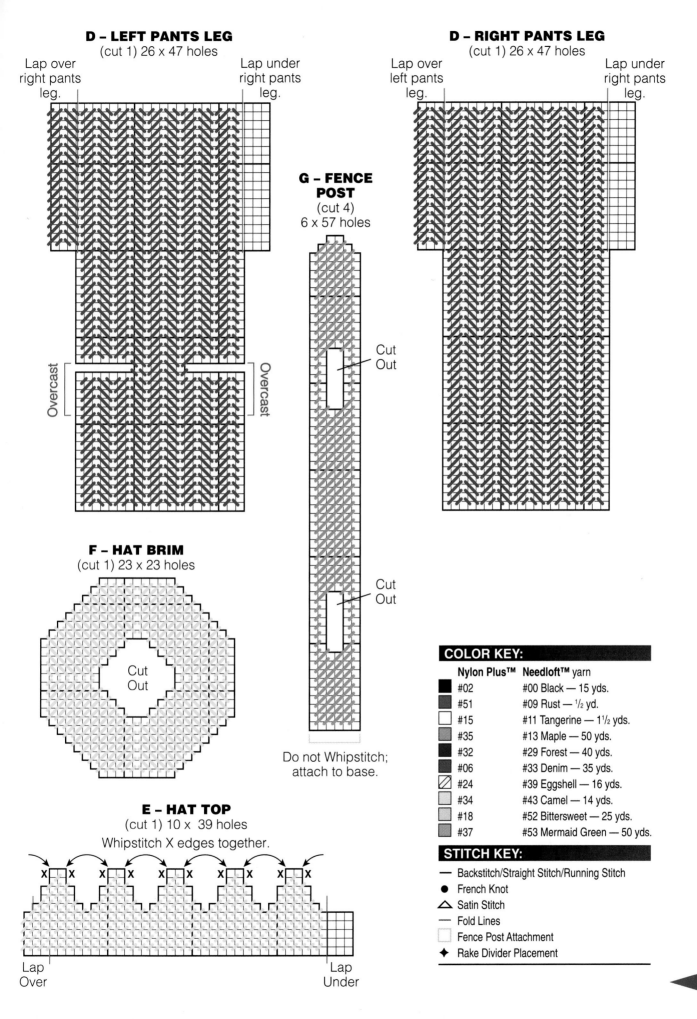

D – LEFT PANTS LEG
(cut 1) 26 x 47 holes

Lap over right pants leg.

Lap under right pants leg.

Overcast

Overcast

D – RIGHT PANTS LEG
(cut 1) 26 x 47 holes

Lap over left pants leg.

Lap under right pants leg.

G – FENCE POST
(cut 4)
6 x 57 holes

Cut Out

Cut Out

Do not Whipstitch; attach to base.

F – HAT BRIM
(cut 1) 23 x 23 holes

Cut Out

E – HAT TOP
(cut 1) 10 x 39 holes
Whipstitch X edges together.

X X   X X   X X   X X   X X

Lap Over

Lap Under

COLOR KEY:

	Nylon Plus™	Needloft™ yarn
■	#02	#00 Black — 15 yds.
■	#51	#09 Rust — ½ yd.
□	#15	#11 Tangerine — 1½ yds.
▨	#35	#13 Maple — 50 yds.
■	#32	#29 Forest — 40 yds.
▨	#06	#33 Denim — 35 yds.
▨	#24	#39 Eggshell — 16 yds.
▨	#34	#43 Camel — 14 yds.
▨	#18	#52 Bittersweet — 25 yds.
▨	#37	#53 Mermaid Green — 50 yds.

STITCH KEY:

— Backstitch/Straight Stitch/Running Stitch
● French Knot
△ Satin Stitch
— Fold Lines
☐ Fence Post Attachment
✦ Rake Divider Placement

101

I – BASE
(cut 2) 42 x 70 holes

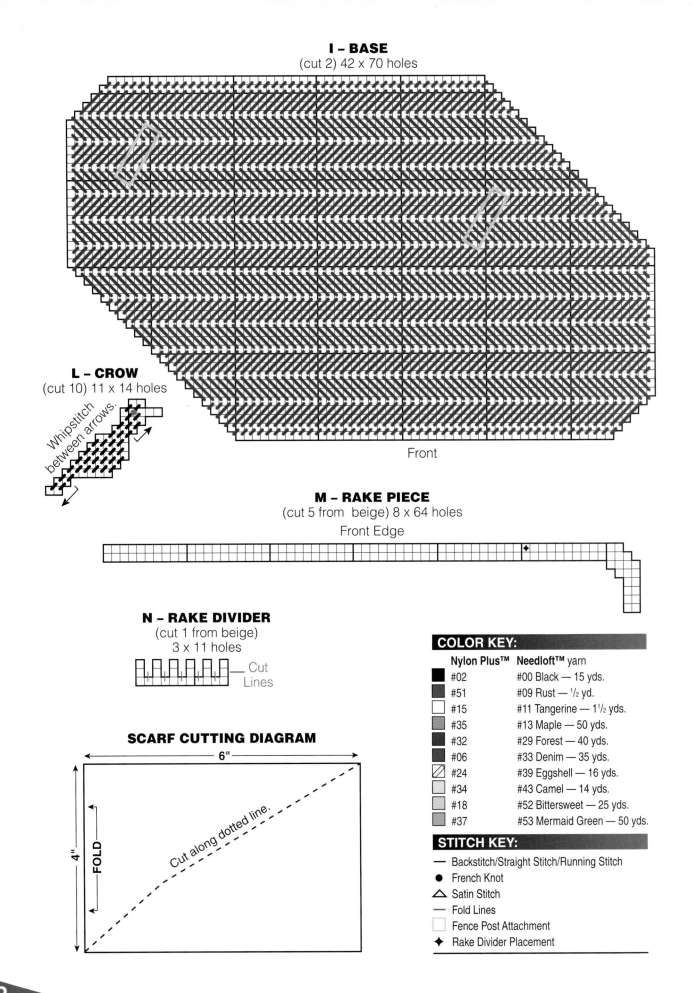

Front

L – CROW
(cut 10) 11 x 14 holes

Whipstitch between arrows.

M – RAKE PIECE
(cut 5 from beige) 8 x 64 holes

Front Edge

N – RAKE DIVIDER
(cut 1 from beige)
3 x 11 holes

— Cut Lines

SCARF CUTTING DIAGRAM

6"

FOLD

4"

Cut along dotted line.

COLOR KEY:

	Nylon Plus™	Needloft™ yarn
■	#02	#00 Black — 15 yds.
■	#51	#09 Rust — ½ yd.
□	#15	#11 Tangerine — 1½ yds.
■	#35	#13 Maple — 50 yds.
■	#32	#29 Forest — 40 yds.
■	#06	#33 Denim — 35 yds.
⊘	#24	#39 Eggshell — 16 yds.
■	#34	#43 Camel — 14 yds.
■	#18	#52 Bittersweet — 25 yds.
■	#37	#53 Mermaid Green — 50 yds.

STITCH KEY:

— Backstitch/Straight Stitch/Running Stitch
● French Knot
△ Satin Stitch
— Fold Lines
□ Fence Post Attachment
◆ Rake Divider Placement

CAROUSEL HORSE DOORSTOP

BY CAROLYN CHRISTMAS

W ith its gilded saddle and gossamer mane, this magical carousel horse tops a weighted base and is perfect for holding even the most elegant doors.

Instructions begin on page 104

SIZE: 11¾" x 16¾" tall; holds a standard-size brick.

SKILL LEVEL: Challenging

MATERIALS: Three sheets of 7-count plastic canvas; Brick; Two 18" lengths of 18-gauge florist wire; Craft glue or glue gun; Heavy metallic braid or cord (for amount see Color Key on page 105); Worsted-weight or plastic canvas yarn (for amounts see Color Key).

CUTTING INSTRUCTIONS:

A: For horse, cut two according to graph.

B: For saddle, cut two according to graph.

C: For pole, cut two according to graph.

D: For brick cover top and bottom, cut one each 22 x 59 holes.

E: For brick cover sides, cut two 20 x 59 holes.

F: For brick cover ends, cut two 20 x 22 holes.

STITCHING INSTRUCTIONS:

NOTE: Measure brick and cover pieces to be sure of fit.

1: Using colors and stitches indicated, work A and B pieces (one each on opposite side of canvas), C and one D (leaving indicated area unworked) pieces according to graphs. Fill in uncoded areas of A pieces using Eggshell and B pieces using Lilac and Continental Stitch. Following pattern established on top D, work E and F pieces. Using metallic braid or cord, Smyrna Cross Stitch (see Stitch Illustration), Backstitch and Straight Stitch, embroider detail on B pieces as indicated on graph.

2: With Purple for seat area of saddle and with braid or cord, Overcast unfinished edges of B pieces as indicated. With Eggshell, Overcast indicated area of each A piece. For each side, with right sides up, hold one B piece over one A piece as indicated; with matching colors, Whipstitch Z edges together.

3: Holding A pieces wrong sides together, with matching colors for legs and ear and with Eggshell, Whipstitch unfinished edges together as indicated. With Lilac, Whipstitch unfinished front and back edges of saddle pieces together.

NOTE: Cut one 1-yd. length of

braid or cord for bridle and reins and one 1-yd. length of braid or 18" length of cord for cinch.

4: For bridle and reins, thread 1-yd. strand of braid or cord in needle and work according to Bridle Diagram as follows: Insert needle from front to back at X, leaving 8" end; following arrow #1, bring thread around to front and insert to back at X; repeat for arrows #2 and #3 at Y. Work a French Knot on back and insert again through to front at X; repeat following arrows #4, #5 and #6 at Y. Work a French Knot on back as at X; follow arrow #7, ending on front at Y. Work a French Knot and insert through to back; insert through to front again at X. Work a French Knot and insert through to back. Remove needle; trim end to 8".

5: For cinch, with 1-yd. strand of braid doubled or with 18" length of cord, insert through front saddle piece from back to front as indicated, leaving 2" end. Go under horse and through back saddle piece from front to back, then from back to front through neighboring indicated hole. Go back under horse and through remaining indicated hole from front to back. Tie ends in knot and trim excess.

NOTE: Cut thirty 15" lengths of Eggshell.

6: For each length of mane and tail, using one 15" strand Eggshell, work Lark's Head Knots as indicated; untwist each strand.

7: Holding C pieces wrong sides together with wires between, with Lilac for ball and with Sandstone, Whipstitch together as indicated, leaving excess wire extending through bottom edges. Inserting visible wire through top D piece at indicated area, with Purple, Whipstitch bottom edge of pole to top D as indicated. Bending wire to fit over sides of brick according to Wire Diagram, place top D over brick; glue wire to brick to stabilize pole.

8: With Purple, Whipstitch D (use unworked piece for bottom), E and F pieces together around brick. Slide open edges of horse over pole. With Lilac and working through all thicknesses, Whipstitch unfinished edges of saddle and horse together. Tie ends of reins together behind pole. ❧

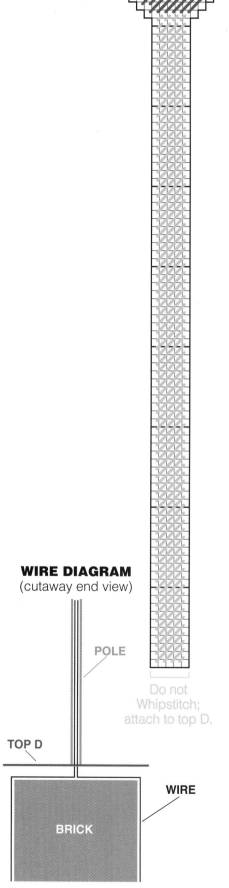

C – POLE
(cut 2)
11 x 90 holes

WIRE DIAGRAM
(cutaway end view)

POLE

Do not Whipstitch; attach to top D.

TOP D

WIRE

BRICK

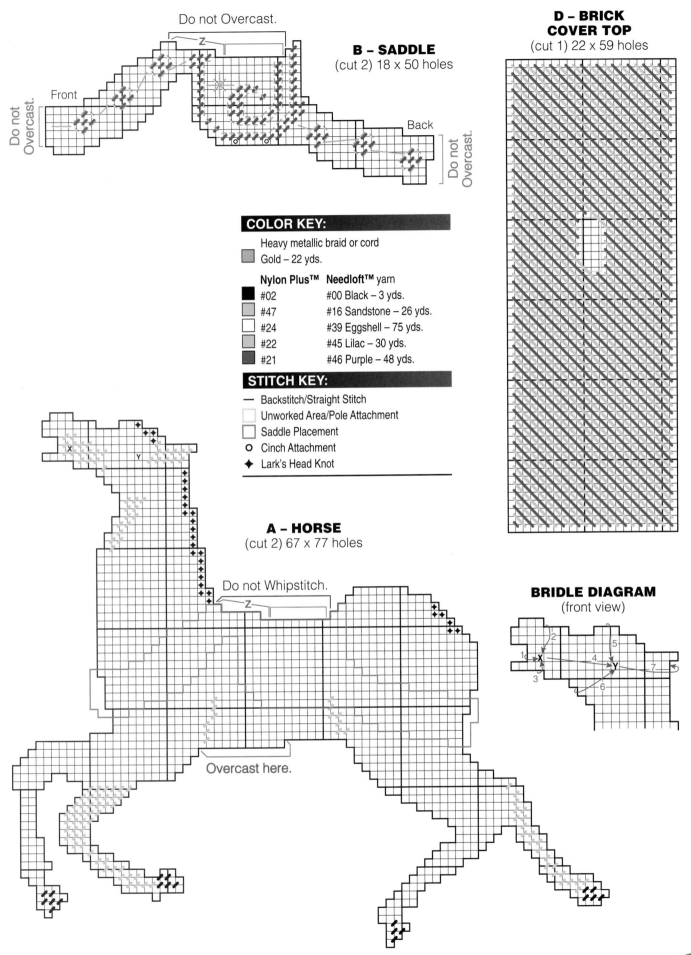

B – SADDLE
(cut 2) 18 x 50 holes

Do not Overcast.

Front

Do not Overcast.

Back

Do not Overcast.

D – BRICK COVER TOP
(cut 1) 22 x 59 holes

COLOR KEY:

Heavy metallic braid or cord
Gold – 22 yds.

Nylon Plus™	Needloft™ yarn
#02	#00 Black – 3 yds.
#47	#16 Sandstone – 26 yds.
#24	#39 Eggshell – 75 yds.
#22	#45 Lilac – 30 yds.
#21	#46 Purple – 48 yds.

STITCH KEY:

— Backstitch/Straight Stitch
☐ Unworked Area/Pole Attachment
☐ Saddle Placement
○ Cinch Attachment
✦ Lark's Head Knot

A – HORSE
(cut 2) 67 x 77 holes

X

Y

Do not Whipstitch.

Z

Overcast here.

BRIDLE DIAGRAM
(front view)

105

A – ANGEL
(cut 2)
46 x 59 holes

SIZE: Worked piece is 7" x 9¾".

SKILL LEVEL: Easy

MATERIALS: One sheet of 7-count plastic canvas; 2 yds. red 1½" (type shown) ribbon; 14" grapevine wreath; Craft glue or glue gun; Worsted-weight or plastic canvas yarn (for amounts see Color Key).

CUTTING INSTRUCTIONS:

A: For angel, cut two according to graph.

B: For arms, cut two according to graph.

STITCHING INSTRUCTIONS:

1: Using colors indicated and Continental Stitch, work one A and B (one on opposite side of canvas) pieces according to graphs. Fill in uncoded areas using White and Continental Stitch. Using Cinnamon and French Knot for eyes and Christmas Red and Backstitch for mouth, embroider A as indicated on graph. With White for sleeves and with Flesh Tone, Overcast unfinished edges of arms.

2: Holding unworked A to wrong side of worked piece, with White for dress and with matching colors, Whipstitch together. Glue one arm to each side of angel as indicated; glue hands together. Wrap ribbon around wreath; tie in bow and trim ends. Glue angel to wreath as shown in photo. ❦

B – ARM
(cut 2) 15 x 23 holes

COLOR KEY:

Nylon Plus™	Needloft™ yarn
#19	#02 Christmas Red – 4 yds.
#15	#11 Tangerine – 6 yds.
#44	#14 Cinnamon – 5 yds.
#31	#27 Holly – 6 yds.
#01	#41 White – 30 yds.
#14	#56 Flesh Tone – 8 yds.

STITCH KEY:

— Backstitch/Straight Stitch
● French Knot
☐ Arm Placement

CHERUB WREATH

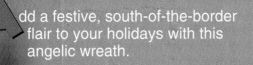

BY
MICHELE
WILCOX

HOLIDAY MEMORIES

BY MICHELE WILCOX

Angels we have... heard on high

Keep photos of your special angels in this pretty holiday photo album. Simply attach the stitched piece to a purchased binder.

SIZE: 7⅝" x 9½", not including ruffle.

SKILL LEVEL: Easy

MATERIALS: ¾ sheet of 7-count plastic canvas; 1 yd. white 1" pregathered ruffle with scallop trim; Craft glue or glue gun; Worsted-weight or plastic canvas yarn (for amounts see Color Key).

CUTTING INSTRUCTIONS:

A: For sampler, cut one 50 x 62 holes.

STITCHING INSTRUCTIONS:

1: Using colors indicated and Continental Stitch, work A according to graph. Fill in uncoded areas using Navy and Continental Stitch; Overcast unfinished edges. Glue ruffle to wrong side as shown in photo. Hang as desired.❦

COLOR KEY:

	Nylon Plus™	Needloft™ yarn
	#41	#19 Straw — 6 yds.
	#45	#31 Navy — 40 yds.
	#05	#36 Baby Blue — 7 yds.
	#01	#41 White — 2½ yds.
	#53	#42 Crimson — 3½ yds.
	#37	#53 Mermaid Green — 4 yds.
	#14	#56 Flesh Tone — 2 yds.

A – SAMPLER
(cut 1) 50 x 62 holes

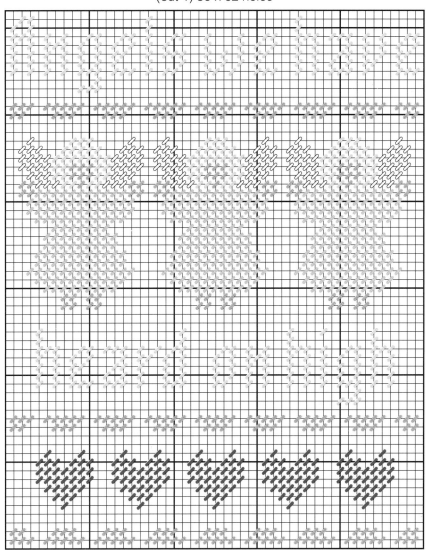

Keep tissues nearby in this cheerful holder, graced with simple, charming images of Mary and Baby Jesus.

Mother & Child

BY MICHELE WILCOX

SIZE: Loosely covers a boutique-style tissue box.

SKILL LEVEL: Easy

MATERIALS: Two sheets of 7-count plastic canvas; Velcro® closure (optional); #3 pearl cotton or six-strand embroidery floss (for amount see Color Key); Worsted-weight or plastic canvas yarn (for amounts see Color Key).

CUTTING INSTRUCTIONS:

A: For top, cut one according to graph.

B: For sides, cut four 31 x 36 holes.

C: For mother, cut one according to graph.

D: For halo, cut one according to graph.

E: For arms, cut two according to graph.

F: For child, cut one according to graph.

G: For optional cover bottom and flap, cut one 31 x 31 holes and one 12 x 31 holes.

STITCHING INSTRUCTIONS:

1: Using colors and stitches indicated, work A-F pieces (work one E on opposite side of canvas) according to graphs. Fill in un-coded areas of D and F using White and Continental Stitch. Using pearl cotton or six strands floss and French Knot (wrap yarn around needle once for child and twice for mother), embroider eyes as indicated on graphs.

2: With matching colors, Overcast unfinished cutout edges of A and unfinished edges of C, D and E pieces. With Tangerine for halo and with White, Overcast unfinished edges of F.

3: With Camel, Whipstitch A and B pieces together, forming cover. For optional cover bottom, Whipstitch unworked G pieces together at one matching edge according to Tissue Cover Assembly Diagram. Whipstitch opposite edge of bottom to one side of cover. Overcast remaining unfinished bottom edges of cover. If desired, glue closure to flap and inside of cover.

4: Glue arms and child to mother as indicated and as shown in photo. Glue halo behind mother's head. Matching bottom edges, glue motif to one side of cover. ❦

COLOR KEY:

	#3 pearl cotton or floss	
■	Black – ½ yd.	

	Nylon Plus™	Needloft™ yarn
	#10	#08 Baby Pink – 2 yds.
	#15	#11 Tangerine – 6 yds.
◨	#25	#20 Lemon – 3 yds.
	#45	#31 Navy – 8 yds.
	#38	#34 Cerulean – 18 yds.
□	#01	#41 White – 4 yds.
	#34	#43 Camel – 72 yds.

STITCH KEY:

● French Knot
□ Arm Placement

C – MOTHER
(cut 1) 26 x 36 holes

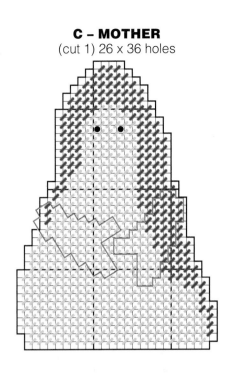

E – ARM
(cut 2)
9 x 12 holes

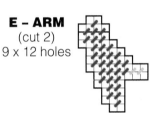

D – HALO
(cut 1)
14 x 16 holes

B – SIDE
(cut 4) 31 x 36 holes

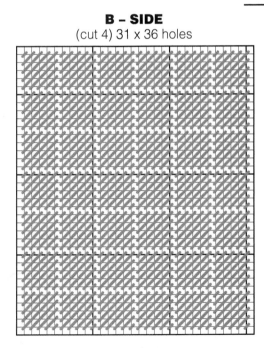

A – TOP
(cut 1) 31 x 31 holes

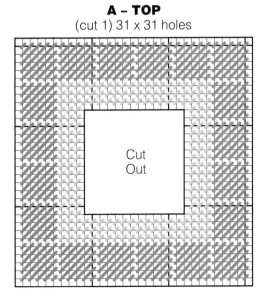

Cut Out

F – CHILD
(cut 1)
11 x 22 holes

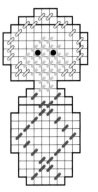

111

FOLK ART ANGEL

BY MICHELE WILCOX

Decorated with Pennsylvania-Dutch flowers and motifs, this sweetheart angel will bring delight to a mantel or tabletop.

Photographed at *Munzesheimer Manor, Mineola, Texas.*

SIZE: 10½" tall.

SKILL LEVEL: Easy

MATERIALS: One sheet of 7-count plastic canvas; One package blonde curly doll hair; 18-20 miniature silk flowers; One 2" Styrofoam® ball; Black and pink acrylic paint; Craft glue or glue gun; Worsted-weight or plastic canvas yarn (for amounts see Color Key).

CUTTING INSTRUCTIONS:

A: For dress, cut one according to graph.

B: For sleeves, cut two according to graph.

C: For hands, cut two according to graph.

D: For wings, cut two according to graph.

STITCHING INSTRUCTIONS:

NOTE: Paint ball pink; let dry. With black, paint eyes and mouth on ball as shown in photo.

1: Using colors indicated and Continental Stitch, work A according to graph. Fill in uncoded areas and work B pieces using Cerulean and Continental Stitch. Using Baby Pink for hands and White for wings and Continental Stitch, work C and D pieces (one each on opposite side of canvas); with matching colors, Overcast unfinished edges as indicated on graph.

2: For dress and each sleeve, folding each piece wrong sides together as indicated, with Cerulean, Whipstitch side edges of each piece together as indicated; Overcast unfinished edges. Holding D pieces right sides together, with White, Whipstitch unfinished edges together.

3: Glue head to top of dress.

Glue sleeves to each side of dress ¼" from top edge as shown. Glue one hand inside each sleeve; glue hands together. With right side of Wings facing front, glue seam to back of dress. Glue hair to top of head and flowers to hair, forming crown.❦

COLOR KEY:

	Nylon Plus™	Needloft™ yarn
#12	#05 Lavender – 3½ yds.
#10	#08 Baby Pink – 2½ yds.
#32	#29 Forest – 8 yds.
#38	#34 Cerulean – 2 oz.
#43	#40 Beige – 1½ yds.
#01	#41 White – 20 yds.
#53	#42 Crimson – 2 yds.

STITCH KEY:

— Fold Lines

D – WING
(cut 2)
21 x 31 holes

Cut Out

Cut Out

Do not Overcast.

B – SLEEVE
(cut 2) 18 x 24 holes

Whipstitch between arrows.

Whipstitch between arrows.

A – DRESS
(cut 1) 52 x 64 holes

Whipstitch between arrows.

Whipstitch between arrows.

C – HAND
(cut 2)
6 x 9 holes

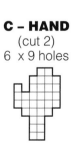

113

SIZE: 3½" x 10½" x 10⅛" tall.

SKILL LEVEL: Easy

MATERIALS: Two sheets of 7-count plastic canvas; Craft glue or glue gun; Worsted-weight or plastic canvas yarn (for amounts see Color Key on page 116).

CUTTING INSTRUCTIONS:
(See graphs on pages 116 & 117.)

A: For front, cut one 25 x 60 holes.

B: For back, cut one according to graph.

C: For ends, cut two 22 x 25 holes.

D: For bottom, cut one 22 x 60 holes.

E: For arms, cut two according to graph.

STITCHING INSTRUCTIONS:

1: Using colors and stitches indicated, work A, B, D and one E piece according to graphs. Substituting Christmas Red for Cerulean and Christmas Green for Christmas Red, work remaining E piece on opposite side of canvas according to graph. Fill in uncoded areas of A and B using White and Continental Stitch. Using Black and French Knot for eyes and Backstitch for mouths, embroider as indicated on graph. Using Christmas Red and Slanted Gobelin Stitch over 2 bars, work C pieces in horizontal rows across narrow width. With matching colors, Overcast unfinished edges of E pieces.

2: With B facing front and matching bottom edges, with Christmas Red, Whipstitch A-D pieces together, forming holder. With matching colors, Overcast unfinished edges. Glue arms to back as shown in photo. ❦

JOY TO THE WORLD

BY MICHELE WILCOX

These cheerfully-clad singers will welcome your guests with candy or other treats. It will even hold your holiday mail.

C – END
(cut 2)
22 x 25 holes

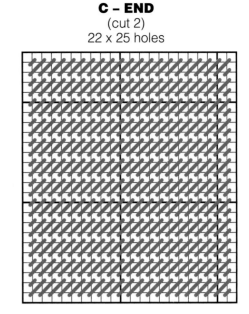

A – FRONT
(cut 1) 25 x 60 holes

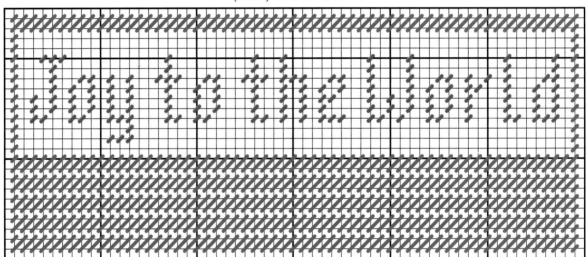

D – BOTTOM
(cut 1) 22 x 60 holes

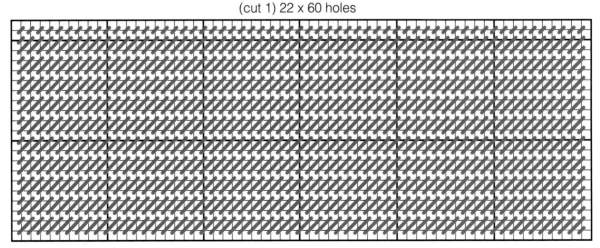

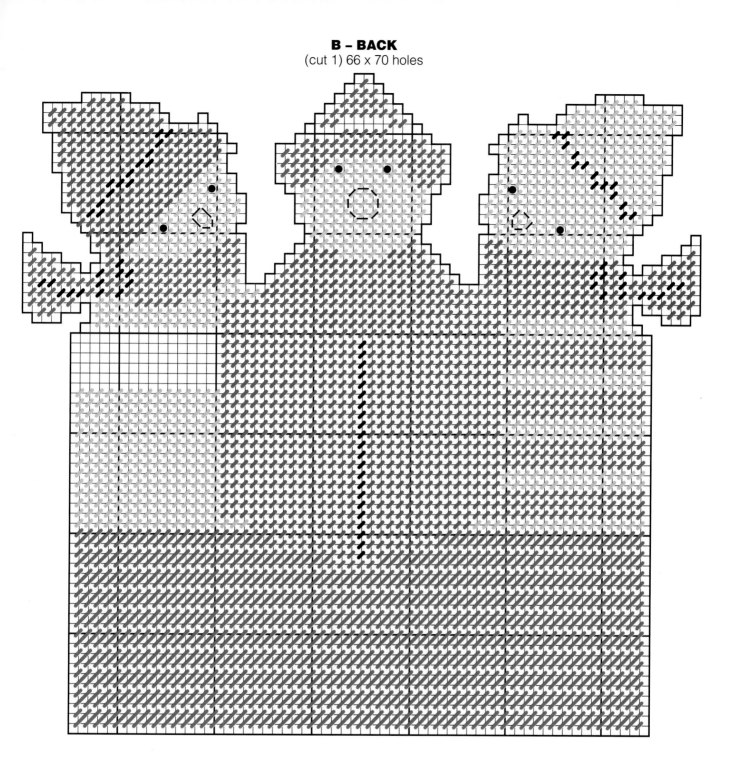

E – ARM
(cut 2) 18 x 24 holes

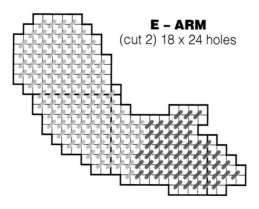

Plastic Canvas

As the days grow shorter, our thoughts turn to family get-togethers and festivities for which we want our homes to be bright, cheerful and warm. Winter is a time for passing an afternoon with a pot of tea and a close friend, writing a newsy card to someone far away, and reminding our loved ones how much we appreciate them. ❄

SENSATIONS

HAPPY
SNOWMAN
BASKET

BY
MICHELE
WILCOX

*F*ill this dancing snowman basket with a selection of special candies, delicious coffees and fine hot chocolate blends and present it to a friend. When the gifts are gone, this cheery winter caddy will hold mail, greeting cards or potpourri.

SIZE: 5½" square x 4¼" tall, not including handle.

SKILL LEVEL: Easy

MATERIALS: 1½ sheets of 7-count plastic canvas; Craft glue or glue gun; #3 pearl cotton or six-strand embroidery floss (for amount see Color Key); Worsted-weight or plastic canvas yarn (for amounts see Color Key).

CUTTING INSTRUCTIONS:

A: For sides, cut four 27 x 36 holes.

B: For bottom, cut one 36 x 36 holes.

C: For handle, cut one 8 x 70 holes and shape ends according to Handle End Graph.

STITCHING INSTRUCTIONS:

1: Using colors indicated and Continental Stitch, work A pieces according to graph. Fill in uncoded areas and work B and C pieces using Denim and Continental Stitch. Using pearl cotton or six strands floss and French Knot (wrap around needle twice for eyes and once for mouths), embroider faces as indicated on graph.

2: With Denim, Overcast unfinished edges of C. Whipstitch A and B pieces together, forming basket; Overcast unfinished edges. Glue handle ends to opposite sides as indicated.✳

COLOR KEY:

#3 pearl cotton or floss
☐ Black – 2½ yds.

Nylon Plus™	Needloft™ yarn
■ #02	#00 Black – 8 yds.
■ #19	#02 Christmas Red – 11 yds.
☐ #06	#33 Denim – 84 yds.
▨ #01	#41 White – 20 yds.
■ #37	#53 Mermaid Green – 12 yds.

STITCH KEY:

● French Knot
☐ Handle Attachment

HANDLE END GRAPH

A – SIDE
(cut 4)
27 x 36 holes

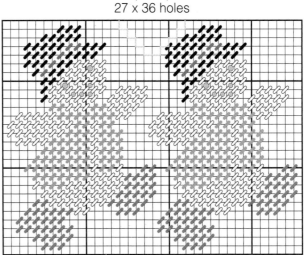

Take time to stitch a gift of love that sends along a heartfelt message. These greeting cards are really two gifts in one — the inserts can be framed for display on a wall or shelf.

ROMANTIC GREETING CARDS

BY
CELIA
LANGE

SIZE: Each insert fits a 5" x 7" needlework greeting card or frame.

SKILL LEVEL: Easy

MATERIALS FOR ONE: ½ sheet of 10-count plastic canvas; 5" x 7" needlework card of choice or mat and frame; Craft glue or glue gun; Medium metallic braid (for amounts see individual Color Keys on pages 123 & 124); #5 pearl cotton or six-strand embroidery floss (for amounts see Color Keys).

CUTTING INSTRUCTIONS:
(See graphs on pages 123 & 124.)

A: For insert, cut one 47 x 69 holes.

STITCHING INSTRUCTIONS:
1: Using braid and pearl cotton or six strands floss in colors indicated and Cross Stitch, work A according to graph of choice. Fill in uncoded area inside indicating line using background color and Cross Stitch, leaving remaining area unworked. Using colors indicated and Backstitch for "Love," Backstitch and French Knot for "With Love" and French Knot, woven Straight Stitch and Couching Stitch (see Stitch Illustration) for "Hearts & Flowers," embroider detail as indicated on graph.

2: Glue insert behind opening in card or frame as desired. Place card under a heavy book to dry. ✳

COUCHING STITCH ILLUSTRATION

COLOR KEY:
Medium metallic braid
- ■ Red – 3 yds.

#5 pearl cotton or floss
- ☐ Background color – 40 yds.
- ■ Dk. Pink – 4 yds.
- ☐ Lt. Pink – 5 yds.
- ■ Dk. Green – 4 yds.
- ☐ Lt. Green – 7 yds.
- ☐ White – 1 yd.

STITCH KEY:
- — Backstitch/Straight Stitch
- ● French Knot
- ⊹ Couching Stitch

A – "HEARTS & FLOWERS" INSERT
(cut 1) 47 x 69 holes

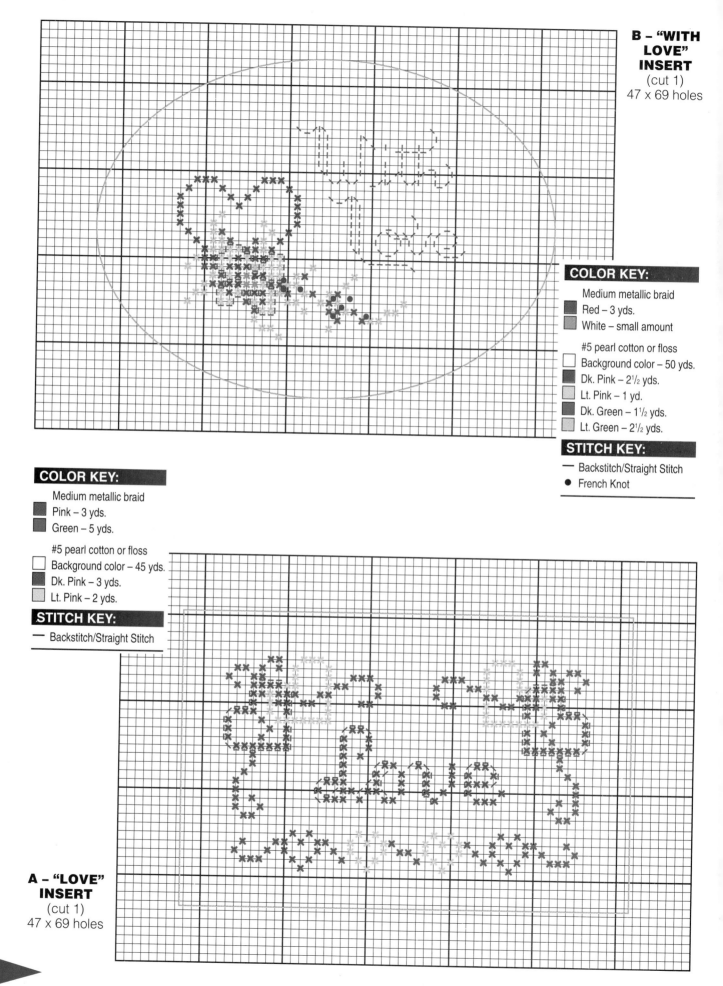

B – "WITH LOVE" INSERT
(cut 1)
47 x 69 holes

COLOR KEY:

Medium metallic braid
Red – 3 yds.
White – small amount

#5 pearl cotton or floss
Background color – 50 yds.
Dk. Pink – 2½ yds.
Lt. Pink – 1 yd.
Dk. Green – 1½ yds.
Lt. Green – 2½ yds.

STITCH KEY:

— Backstitch/Straight Stitch
● French Knot

COLOR KEY:

Medium metallic braid
Pink – 3 yds.
Green – 5 yds.

#5 pearl cotton or floss
Background color – 45 yds.
Dk. Pink – 3 yds.
Lt. Pink – 2 yds.

STITCH KEY:

— Backstitch/Straight Stitch

A – "LOVE" INSERT
(cut 1)
47 x 69 holes

Rose Potpourri Dish

BY TERESA S. HANNAWAY

*R*eminiscent of antique pewter and glass potpourri holders, this beautiful floral design features cutout areas to allow your favorite scent to subtly perfume your home.

Instructions begin on page 126

SIZE: 2¾" x 7¼" x 8⅜".

SKILL LEVEL: Average

MATERIALS: Three sheets of 7-count plastic canvas; Six plastic baseball card protectors or one plastic notebook cover; Six 12" x 3-mm. white chenille stems; Craft glue or glue gun; Worsted-weight or plastic canvas yarn (for amounts see Color Key).

CUTTING INSTRUCTIONS:

A: For lid motif, cut one according to graph.

B: For lid rim, cut one according to graph.

C: For lid lip pieces, cut six 3 x 24 holes.

D: For box sides, cut six according to graph.

E: For box bottom, cut one according to graph.

STITCHING INSTRUCTIONS:

1: Using colors and stitches indicated, work A, D and E pieces according to graphs. Using Plum and French Knot for centers and Backstitch for outlines, embroider flower detail as indicated on graph. With Aqua, Overcast unfinished cutout edges of D pieces.

NOTE: Cut chenille stems into six 4⅛" and six 3" lengths.

2: Glue chenille stems to inside and outside edges of B. Gluing yarn in place as you work and covering completely, with Aqua, wrap yarn around B.

3: With Eggshell, Whipstitch short ends of C pieces together, forming lid lip. Glue lid lip to wrong side of B. Glue A to top of B as shown in photo. With Aqua, Whipstitch short edges of D pieces together, forming box side. With right side of E on inside, Whipstitch box side and E together; Overcast unfinished edges of box.

NOTE: Cut clear plastic into six 2¼" x 3⅝" pieces.

4: Glue edges of one clear plastic piece to inside of box behind each cutout.✵

A – LID MOTIF
(cut 1)
46 x 49 holes

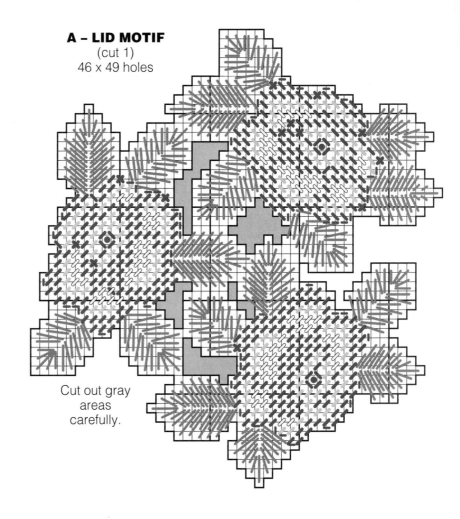

Cut out gray areas carefully.

*S*cent your home with potpourri in this old-fashioned dish.

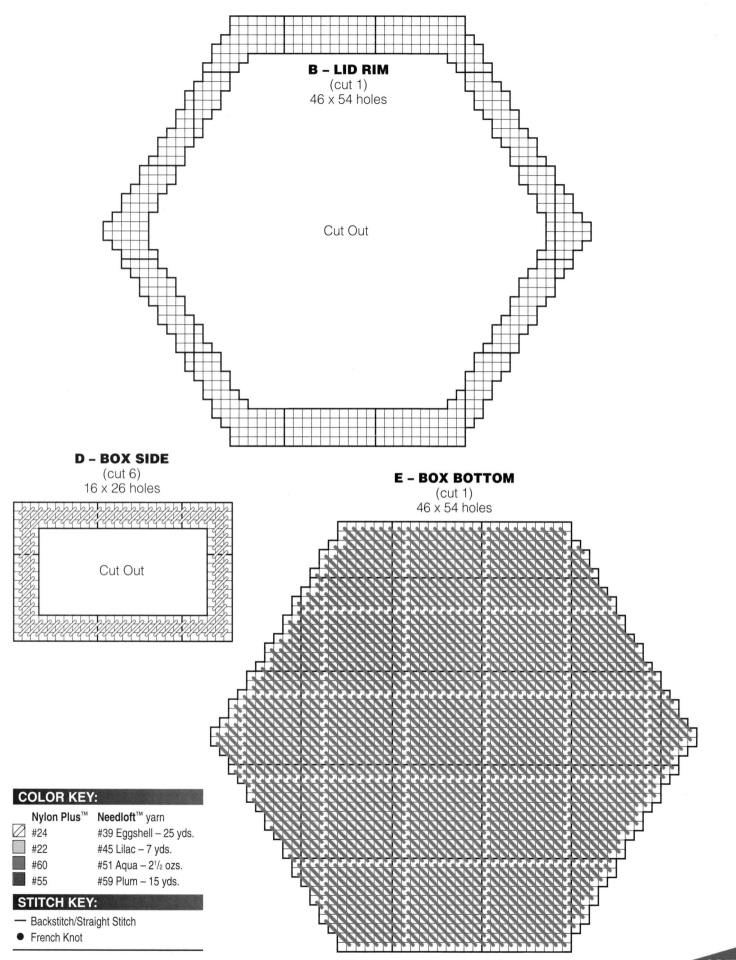

B – LID RIM
(cut 1)
46 x 54 holes

Cut Out

D – BOX SIDE
(cut 6)
16 x 26 holes

Cut Out

E – BOX BOTTOM
(cut 1)
46 x 54 holes

COLOR KEY:

	Nylon Plus™	Needloft™ yarn
⧄	#24	#39 Eggshell – 25 yds.
	#22	#45 Lilac – 7 yds.
	#60	#51 Aqua – 2½ ozs.
	#55	#59 Plum – 15 yds.

STITCH KEY:

— Backstitch/Straight Stitch
● French Knot

TOP STITCH PATTERN GUIDE

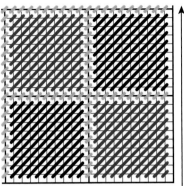

Continue established pattern up and across entire piece, omitting Continental Stitches at outer edges.

BOARD ASSEMBLY DIAGRAM

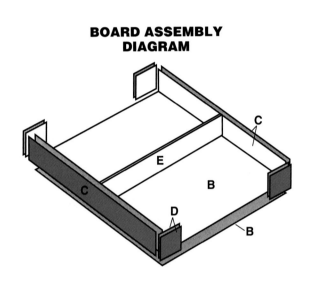

DRAWER INTERIOR ASSEMBLY DIAGRAM

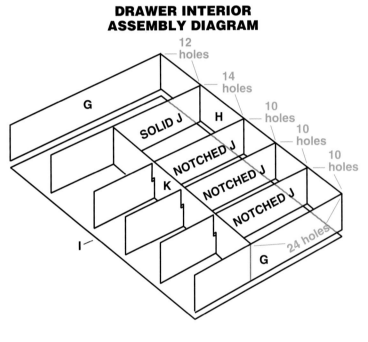

J – NOTCHED SHORT PARTITION
(cut 6)
11 x 38 holes
Top

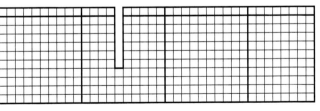

K – LONG PARTITION
(cut 2)
11 x 43 holes
Top

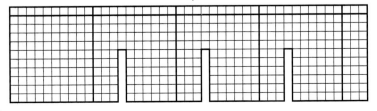

Leave 6-hole overhang at each end.

DRAWER FRONT ASSEMBLY DIAGRAM

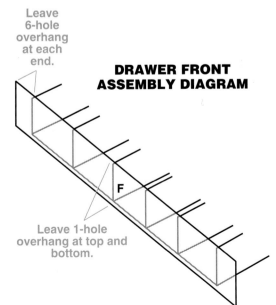

Leave 1-hole overhang at top and bottom.

PLAYING PIECES

CUTTING INSTRUCTIONS:

A: For kings, cut four according to graph.

B: For queens, cut four according to graph.

C: For bishops, cut eight according to graph.

D: For knights, cut eight according to graph.

E: For castles, cut eight according to graph.

F: For pawns, cut thirty-two according to graph.

G: For base tops, cut sixty-four according to graph.

H: For base bottoms, cut thirty-two according to graph.

I: For checkers, cut forty-eight according to graph.

STITCHING INSTRUCTIONS:

1: For chess pieces, using metallic cord and stitches indicated, work A, B, C, D (four on opposite side of canvas), E and F pieces according to graphs. Fill in uncoded areas of half the pieces and work half of all G and H pieces using Eggshell and remaining half using Black and Continental Stitch. Using cord and Straight Stitch, embroider detail on C and D pieces as indicated on graphs.

2: With matching colors, Whipstitch one G and each A-F piece together according to Chess Piece Assembly Diagram. Holding matching pieces wrong sides together, Whipstitch remaining edges of each playing piece together. Holding one H piece and base tops wrong sides together (see diagram), Whipstitch together.

3: For checkers, using Burgundy and stitches indicated, work half the I pieces according to graph; substituting Black for Burgundy, work remaining pieces according to graph. To finish each piece, holding two matching-color pieces wrong sides together, with cord, Whipstitch together.❄

I – CHECKER
(cut 48)
7 x 7 holes

A – KING
(cut 4)
7 x 15 holes

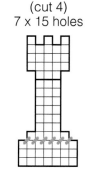

B – QUEEN
(cut 4)
7 x 15 holes

C – BISHOP
(cut 8)
6 x 13 holes

D – KNIGHT
(cut 8)
11 x 14 holes

CHESS PIECE ASSEMBLY DIAGRAM

E – CASTLE
(cut 8)
7 x 11 holes

F – PAWN
(cut 32)
7 x 9 holes

G – BASE TOP
(cut 64)
3 x 7 holes

H – BASE BOTTOM
(cut 32)
7 x 7 holes

131

Victorian
FAN COASTERS

BY TERRY A. RICIOLI

*A*s snow blankets the world, cozy up with a good book and a cup of tea. These feminine coasters will protect your table-tops from moisture. And the set, with its lacy, pearl-trimmed holder, is a delightful decorating accent.

SIZE: Holder is 6½" x 4¾" tall, not including lace; each Coaster is 4¾" x 5¾".

SKILL LEVEL: Average

MATERIALS: 1½ sheets of 7-count plastic canvas; ⅔ yd. rose 1" pregathered lace; ⅔ yd. burgundy ¼" picot-edged satin ribbon; 14 rose ½" ribbon roses; 1 yd. string of 3-mm. pearls; Craft glue or glue gun; Worsted-weight or plastic canvas yarn (for amounts see Color Key).

CUTTING INSTRUCTIONS:

A: For holder side, cut two according to graph.

B: For holder end top pieces, cut two 9 x 23 holes.

C: For holder end bottom pieces, cut two 8 x 9 holes.

D: For coasters, cut four according to graph.

STITCHING INSTRUCTIONS:

1: Using colors and stitches indicated, work A, B and D pieces according to graphs. Fill in uncoded areas and work C pieces using Lavender and Continental Stitch.

2: Using Burgundy and Running Stitch, embroider detail on coasters as indicated on graph. With Burgundy for top edges and with matching colors as shown in photo, Overcast unfinished edges of coasters.

NOTES: Cut six 4" lengths of ribbon. Cut four 3½" and four 4" lengths of pearl string.

3: Keeping ribbon flat and working center lengths last, thread ends of 4" lengths of ribbon from front to back through each A piece as indicated, and glue in place on wrong side. With Burgundy, Whipstitch A, B and C pieces together according to Coaster Holder Assembly Diagram. Overcast unfinished top and bottom edges of holder.

4: Glue lace around inside top edge. Placing shorter lengths on top, glue pearls and ribbon roses to each side of holder as shown. ❋

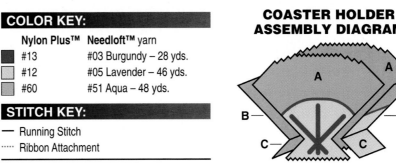

COLOR KEY:

Nylon Plus™	Needloft™ yarn
#13	#03 Burgundy – 28 yds.
#12	#05 Lavender – 46 yds.
#60	#51 Aqua – 48 yds.

STITCH KEY:

— Running Stitch

···· Ribbon Attachment

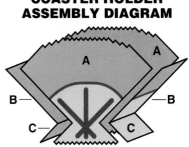

COASTER HOLDER ASSEMBLY DIAGRAM

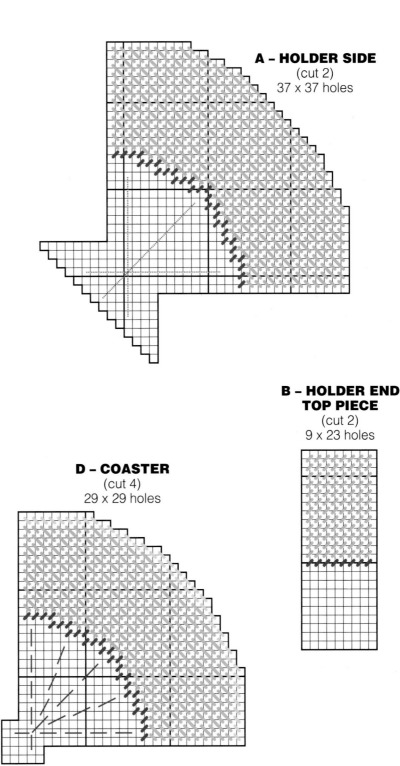

A – HOLDER SIDE
(cut 2)
37 x 37 holes

D – COASTER
(cut 4)
29 x 29 holes

B – HOLDER END TOP PIECE
(cut 2)
9 x 23 holes

Highlight a vanity or dressing table with this floral trio. A frame for a treasured photo, an elegant Victorian fan, and a tiny trinket box will create a designer look for the boudoir.

Roses in the Snow

BY JANICE HOPKINS

SIZE: Fan is 8⅞" x 10¼", not including lace; Frame is 6¼" x 8¼" and holds a 5" x 7" photo; Trinket Box is 2⅞" x 3" x 1¼" tall.

SKILL LEVEL: Average

MATERIALS: Two sheets of 7-count plastic canvas; Two 3" plastic canvas hearts; ⅓ yd. white ½" pregathered lace; ½ yd. red ⅜" picot-edged satin ribbon; 1 yd. red ¾" pregathered lace; Sewing needle and matching color thread or craft glue or glue gun; Raffia straw (for amounts see Color Key); Worsted-weight or plastic canvas yarn (for amount see Color Key).

CUTTING INSTRUCTIONS:
(See graphs on pages 135 & 136.)

A: For Fan, cut one according to graph.

B: For Frame front, cut one according to graph.

C: For Frame back, cut one 41 x 55 holes and cut out slot according to Frame Slot Graph.

D: For Frame support, cut one 27 x 49 holes.

E: For Frame base, cut one 10 x 41 holes.

F: For box top and bottom, use canvas hearts.

G: For box side pieces, cut two 7 x 30 holes.

H: For lid lip pieces, cut two 3 x 27 holes.

STITCHING INSTRUCTIONS:

1: For Fan, using Red raffia and stitches indicated (see Rose Illustration), work roses and buds only on A according to graph. Fill in uncoded areas using White and Continental Stitch, working under edges of buds and roses and over ends of base stitches. Using Christmas Green raffia and Straight Stitch, embroider leaves and stems as indicated on graph. (**NOTE:** For thinner stems and to help them curve, twist raffia strand by turning needle a few times.)

2: With White, Overcast unfinished edges of fan; using White and Straight Stitch, embroider section dividers as indicated. Sew or glue red lace around outer edge, and tie ribbon into a bow around handle as shown in photo.

3: For Frame, follow Step 1 with B piece. With White, Overcast unfinished cutout edges. Whipstitch one short edge of D to center of bottom bar of slot on C.

Holding unworked C to wrong side of B with slot at top, Whipstitch side and top edges together. Working through all thicknesses, Whipstitch bottom edges and one long edge of E together; Overcast unfinished edges of base, catching end of support at center to join.

4: For Trinket Box, follow Step 1 with top F. Using White and Continental Stitch, work G and bottom F pieces. Using White and Long Stitch over narrow width, work H pieces. Whipstitch short ends of G pieces together, forming side; repeat with H pieces, forming lid lip. Overcast unfinished edges of all pieces. Matching side seams to points on heart, tack or glue box sides to bottom and lid lip just inside outer edge of lid top. Sew or glue white lace to lid top as shown in photo.❄

F – BOX TOP
(use canvas heart)

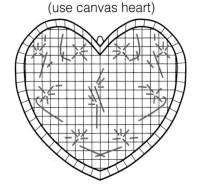

Here's a sweetheart box for even your tiniest trinkets.

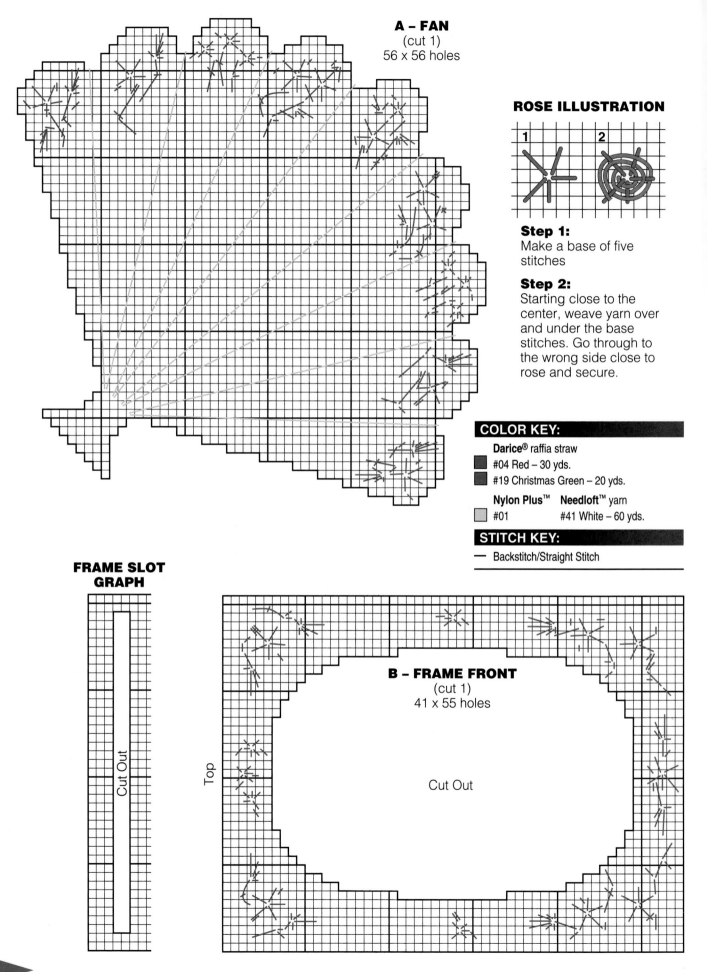

A – FAN
(cut 1)
56 x 56 holes

ROSE ILLUSTRATION

Step 1:
Make a base of five stitches

Step 2:
Starting close to the center, weave yarn over and under the base stitches. Go through to the wrong side close to rose and secure.

COLOR KEY:

Darice® raffia straw

■ #04 Red – 30 yds.
■ #19 Christmas Green – 20 yds.

Nylon Plus™   Needloft™ yarn

□ #01   #41 White – 60 yds.

STITCH KEY:

— Backstitch/Straight Stitch

FRAME SLOT GRAPH

Cut Out

Top

B – FRAME FRONT
(cut 1)
41 x 55 holes

Cut Out

HIDE & SEEK

BY TRUDY BATH SMITH

S urprise the pet lover on
your gift list with this precious puppy
tissue cover. He peeks out each time the
lid is raised for a tissue.

Instructions begin on
page 138

SIZE: Holds a boutique-style tissue box.

SKILL LEVEL: Average

MATERIALS: Two sheets of 7-count plastic canvas; ¼ sheet of white 7-count plastic canvas; Two 12-mm. dog eyes without shank; Craft glue or glue gun; Metallic cord (for amount see Color Key); Worsted-weight or plastic canvas yarn (for amounts see Color Key).

CUTTING INSTRUCTIONS:

NOTE: Use white canvas for lid lining.

A: For box sides, cut four 30 x 40 holes.

B: For box bottom, cut one 30 x 30 holes.

C: For lid top and lining, cut one from each color 32 x 32 holes.

D: For lid sides, cut four 6 x 32 holes.

E: For bow loops, cut two 4 x 34 holes.

F: For bow knot, cut one 4 x 18 holes.

G: For dog head, cut one according to graph.

H: For dog muzzle, cut one according to graph.

I: For dog paws, cut two according to graph.

J: For support, cut one according to graph.

K: For flap, cut one according to graph.

STITCHING INSTRUCTIONS:

1: For box, using colors and stitches indicated, work A, clear C and D pieces according to graphs. With White, Whipstitch A and unworked B pieces together, forming box. Holding unworked C to wrong side of worked piece and working through all thicknesses, Whipstitch C and D pieces together, forming lid. Overcast unfinished edges of box and lid. With White, loosely tack one lid side to box at two corners so lid can be opened but will not come off.

2: For bow, using Pink and Slanted Gobelin over narrow width, work E and F pieces; with Forest, Overcast unfinished long edges. With Pink, Whipstitch short ends of each E together, forming loops, and Whipstitch short ends of F together, forming knot. Glue Whipstitched end of each E piece inside F to form bow. Glue bow at an angle to center top of lid.

3: For dog, using colors indicated and Continental Stitch, work G and H pieces according to graphs. Fill in uncoded areas and work I pieces using White and Continental Stitch. With Black for ears, Gray for bottom edges of muzzle as shown in photo and with matching colors, Overcast unfinished edges of G-I pieces. Using Black and Satin Stitch, embroider nose on muzzle as indicated.

4: To assemble, with White, Whipstitch long straight edge of unworked K and bottom of unworked J together according to Dog Assembly Diagram; Overcast unfinished side edges of J. Leaving bottom edge of head free, glue paws and head to support (see diagram). Glue eyes and muzzle to head as shown. Glue top ends of support centered inside front edge of lid at seam. To hold lid open, insert flap between box and tissue box.❈

DOG ASSEMBLY DIAGRAM

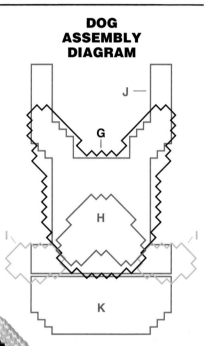

A precious puppy hides under this beribboned box lid.

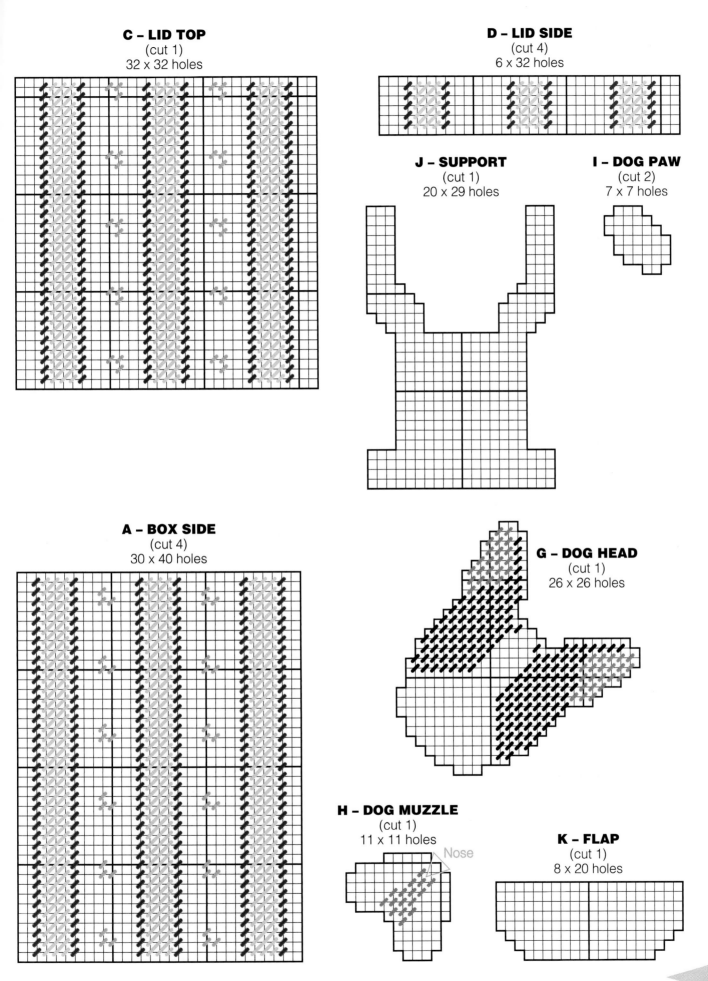

C – LID TOP
(cut 1)
32 x 32 holes

D – LID SIDE
(cut 4)
6 x 32 holes

J – SUPPORT
(cut 1)
20 x 29 holes

I – DOG PAW
(cut 2)
7 x 7 holes

A – BOX SIDE
(cut 4)
30 x 40 holes

G – DOG HEAD
(cut 1)
26 x 26 holes

H – DOG MUZZLE
(cut 1)
11 x 11 holes

Nose

K – FLAP
(cut 1)
8 x 20 holes

139

COUNTRY COW CATCHALL

BY MICHELE WILCOX

*W*ant to add a fresh country touch to your breakfast table? This clever cow will keep your napkins handy and smiles *moo*ving right along.

SIZE: 4⅝" x 5¾" x about 8½" tall.

SKILL LEVEL: Easy

MATERIALS: 1½ sheets of 7-count plastic canvas; ⅝" gold liberty bell; 12" jute cord; Craft glue or glue gun; Worsted-weight or plastic canvas yarn (for amounts see Color Key).

CUTTING INSTRUCTIONS:

A: For head, cut one according to graph.

B: For muzzle, cut one according to graph.

C: For ends, cut two according to graph.

D: For sides, cut two 24 x 36 holes.

E: For bottom, cut one 26 x 36 holes.

F: For leg backs, cut four according to graph.

STITCHING INSTRUCTIONS:

1: Using colors indicated and Continental Stitch, work A-D and F pieces according to graphs. Fill in uncoded areas and work E using White and Continental Stitch. With White for ears and with matching colors, Overcast unfinished edges of A and B pieces. Using Black and French Knot for eyes and nostrils and Red and Backstitch for mouth, embroider as indicated on graphs.

2: To join leg backs to ends, holding one F and leg area on each C piece wrong sides together, with matching colors, Whipstitch together as indicated. With White, Overcast remaining unfinished edges of C pieces.

3: With White, Whipstitch D and E pieces together according to Catchall Assembly Diagram; Overcast unfinished edges. Glue assembly and ends together as indicated and according to diagram. Glue muzzle to head as indicated; leaving side edges loose, glue head to one end as shown in photo. Tie bell to center of jute cord; tie ends of cord around head as shown and trim ends.

NOTE: Cut one 4", one 8" and three 15" lengths of Black.

4: For tail, holding 15" lengths of Black together, tie 8" length around center. Fold in half at tie and braid (hold two lengths together) about 2". Tie 4" length at end to secure; trim ends to 1". Thread ends of top tie through to wrong side of back end as indicated; tie in knot and trim ends. ✳

COLOR KEY:

Nylon Plus™	Needloft™ yarn
#02	#00 Black – 28 yds.
#20	#01 Red – 2 yds.
#33	#18 Tan – 1 yd.
#01	#41 White – 90 yds.
#14	#56 Flesh Tone – 3 yds.

STITCH KEY:

— Backstitch/Straight Stitch
● French Knot
□ Muzzle Placement
— Sides & Bottom Placement
X Tail Attachment

C – END
(cut 2) 30 x 38 holes

D – SIDE
(cut 2) 24 x 36 holes
Top

B – MUZZLE
(cut 1) 8 x 12 holes

F – LEG BACK
(cut 4)
9 x 10 holes

Whipstitch between arrows.

Whipstitch leg backs between arrows.

A – HEAD
(cut 1) 27 x 28 holes

CATCHALL ASSEMBLY DIAGRAM

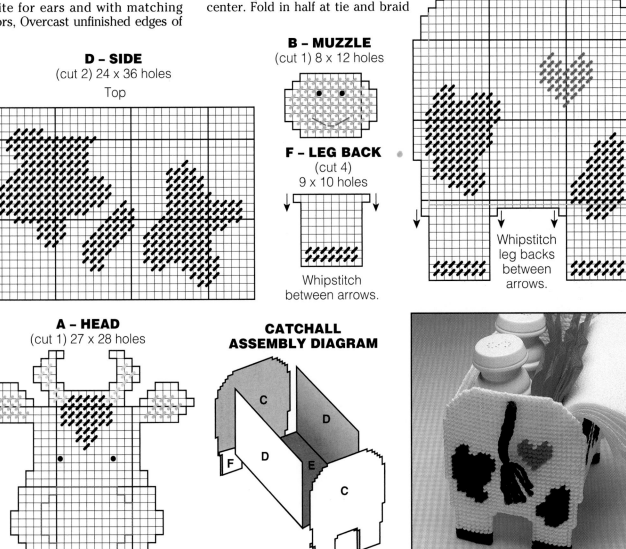

I ♥ EWE

BY MICHELE WILCOX

This tissue holder imparts a sweet and simple sentiment in pretty, cheery colors. It's the perfect gift for a college student, nursing home resident or anyone else you love.

SIZE: Loosely covers a boutique-style tissue box.
SKILL LEVEL: Easy
MATERIALS: Two sheets of 7-count plastic canvas; Velcro® closure (optional); Craft glue or glue gun (optional); Six-strand embroidery floss (for amount see Color Key); Worsted-weight or plastic canvas yarn (for amounts see Color Key).

CUTTING INSTRUCTIONS:
A: For top, cut one according to graph.
B: For sides, cut four 31 x 36 holes.
C: For optional cover bottom and flap, cut one 31 x 31 holes and one 12 x 31 holes.

STITCHING INSTRUCTIONS:
1: Using colors and stitches indicated, work two B pieces according to each graph. Fill in uncoded areas and work A using Royal and Continental Stitch. Using six strands floss and French Knot, embroider eyes as indicated on graph. With Pink, Overcast unfinished cutout edges of A.
2: Alternating sides, with Royal, Whipstitch A and B pieces together, forming cover.

For optional cover bottom, Whipstitch C pieces together at one matching edge (see Assembly Diagram); Whipstitch opposite edge of bottom to one side of tissue cover. Overcast remaining unfinished bottom edges of cover. If desired, glue closure to flap and inside of cover.✳

A – TOP
(cut 1)
31 x 31 holes

Cut Out

TISSUE COVER ASSEMBLY DIAGRAM

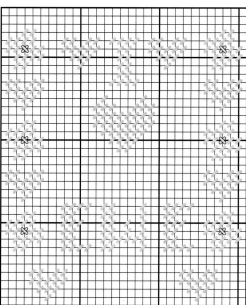

TISSUE COVER SIDE

Whipstitch here.

BOTTOM

FLAP

Whipstitch here.

B – SIDE 1
(cut 2)
31 x 36 holes

B – SIDE 2
(cut 2)
31 x 36 holes

143

*F*ill this cute kitty with cedar chips, lavender or other scent and hang in a closet or cabinet.

B – BODY FRONT & BACK
(cut 1 each)
26 x 35 holes

Kitten SACHET
BY CAROLE RODGERS

A – HEAD
(cut 1)
13 x 16 holes

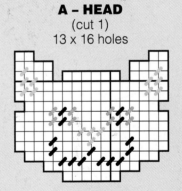

SIZE: 4" x 5½".

SKILL LEVEL: Easy

MATERIALS: ½ sheet of 7-count plastic canvas; ½ yd. green ⅛" satin ribbon; ½" gold liberty bell; 2½" x 5" scrap of netting; Sewing needle and white thread; Two tablespoons cedar chips or potpourri; Craft glue or glue gun; Six-strand embroidery floss (for amount see Color Key); Worsted-weight or plastic canvas yarn (for amounts see Color Key).

CUTTING INSTRUCTIONS:

A: For head, cut one according to graph.

B: For body front and back, cut one each according to graph.

STITCHING INSTRUCTIONS:

1: Using colors indicated and Continental Stitch, work A and one B (leaving indicated area unworked) according to graphs. Fill in uncoded areas using Eggshell and Continental Stitch. Using six strands floss and Backstitch, embroider paws as indicated on graph. With Eggshell, Overcast unfinished edges of A.

2: Folding netting in half crosswise and allowing ¼" for seam, sew edges together, stuffing with cedar chips or potpourri before closing. Holding unworked B to wrong side of worked piece with netting between, with Eggshell, Whipstitch together.

NOTE: Cut satin ribbon into one 3" and one 15" length.

3: Slide bell onto 3" length of ribbon; glue ends of ribbon behind chin on A. Glue head to body as indicated. Tie 15" ribbon into a bow around tail as shown in photo.❈

COLOR KEY:

Embroidery floss
Brown – 1 yd.

Nylon Plus™	Needloft™ yarn
#02	#00 Black – 1 yd.
#11	#07 Pink – 1 yd.
#57	#23 Fern – small amount
#24	#39 Eggshell – 18 yds.
#34	#43 Camel – 3 yds.

STITCH KEY:

— Backstitch/Straight Stitch
☐ Unworked Area/Head Placement

Serve up lots of love to family and friends with this coordinated table setting. It's complete with place mat, basket, trivet and coaster.

WOVEN HEARTS

BY TRUDY BATH SMITH

SIZE: Place Mat is 13¼" x 19⅜"; Trivet is 8⅜" x 8⅝"; Basket is 4⅝" x 11"; Coaster is 3¾" x 4".

SKILL LEVEL: Average

MATERIALS FOR ONE OF EACH: 4½ sheets of 5-count plastic canvas; Metallic cord (for amount see individual Color Keys on pages 149 & 150); Worsted-weight or plastic canvas yarn (for amounts see individual Color Keys).

CUTTING INSTRUCTIONS:
(See graphs on pages 149 & 150.)

A: For Place Mat, cut two 65 x 95 holes.

B: For Trivet, cut two 41 x 42 holes.

C: For Basket sides, cut twelve according to graph.

D: For Basket bottom, cut one according to graph.

E: For Coaster, cut two according to graph.

STITCHING INSTRUCTIONS:

NOTE: Use two strands held together except for Long Stitches.

1: Using colors and stitches indicated, work one A, one B, six C and one E pieces according to graphs. Fill in uncoded areas around small hearts on A using Cerulean and Continental Stitch. Using desired color and Long Stitch, weave through large heart stitches on worked pieces.

2: For Place Mat and Trivet, holding matching unworked piece to wrong side of worked piece, with Royal Dark, Whipstitch to-gether. For Coaster, holding unworked E to wrong side of worked piece, with metallic cord, Whipstitch together.

3: For Basket, holding one unworked C to wrong side of each worked piece and working through all thicknesses, with cord, Whip-stitch side edges together as indicated on graph. Whipstitch sides and unworked D together. Whipstitch unfinished top edges together. ✣

E – COASTER
(cut 2)
18 x 19 holes

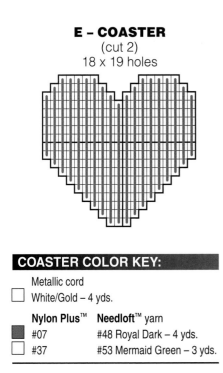

COASTER COLOR KEY:	
Metallic cord	
☐ White/Gold – 4 yds.	
Nylon Plus™	**Needloft**™ yarn
■ #07	#48 Royal Dark – 4 yds.
☐ #37	#53 Mermaid Green – 3 yds.

TRIVET COLOR KEY:	
Nylon Plus™	**Needloft**™ yarn
☐ #12	#05 Lavender – 16 yds.
☐ #24	#39 Eggshell – 28 yds.
■ #07	#48 Royal Dark – 25 yds.
☐ #37	#53 Mermaid Green – 20 yds.

B – TRIVET
(cut 2)
41 x 42 holes

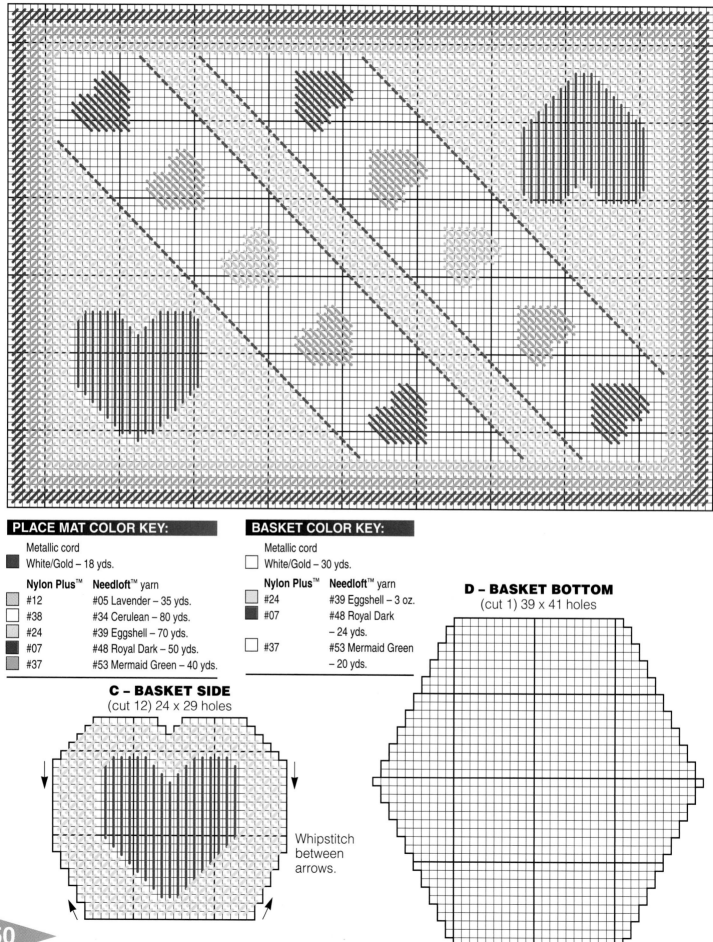

A – PLACE MAT (cut 2) 65 x 95 holes

PLACE MAT COLOR KEY:

Metallic cord
■ White/Gold – 18 yds.

Nylon Plus™	Needloft™ yarn
#12	#05 Lavender – 35 yds.
#38	#34 Cerulean – 80 yds.
#24	#39 Eggshell – 70 yds.
#07	#48 Royal Dark – 50 yds.
#37	#53 Mermaid Green – 40 yds.

BASKET COLOR KEY:

Metallic cord
☐ White/Gold – 30 yds.

Nylon Plus™	Needloft™ yarn
#24	#39 Eggshell – 3 oz.
#07	#48 Royal Dark – 24 yds.
#37	#53 Mermaid Green – 20 yds.

C – BASKET SIDE
(cut 12) 24 x 29 holes

Whipstitch between arrows.

D – BASKET BOTTOM
(cut 1) 39 x 41 holes

Create a feeling of warmth and good cheer in your home with a garland for fireplace or doorway, a fireplace match holder, and a candy jar brightener — decorated with smiling snowmen, ice skates and colorful mittens.

Winter Memories

BY MICHELE WILCOX

Instructions begin on page 152

SIZE: Snowman motif is 3⅞" x 4"; mitten motif is 4½" x 5"; skate motif is 3⅞" x 7½"; bow motif is 3¾" x 4⅜".

SKILL LEVEL: Easy

GARLAND

MATERIALS FOR ONE OF EACH
MOTIF: One sheet of 7-count plastic canvas; Brown twisted paper ribbon; Silk dried rose buds or flowers and baby's breath (optional); Craft glue or glue gun; #3 pearl cotton or six-strand embroidery floss (for amount see Color Key); Worsted-weight or plastic canvas yarn (for amounts see Color Key).

NOTE: For longer garland, determine desired length and number of motifs before purchasing materials.

CUTTING INSTRUCTIONS:
A: For bow motif, cut one according to graph.

B: For snowman motif, cut one according to graph.

C: For skates motif, cut two according to graph.

D: For mittens motif, cut two according to graph.

STITCHING INSTRUCTIONS:
1: Using colors indicated and Continental Stitch, work A-D pieces according to graphs. Fill in uncoded areas using Eggshell and Continental Stitch. Using pearl cotton or six strands floss and French Knot, embroider eyes and mouth on snowman as indicated on graph.

2: With Denim for mittens and with matching colors, Overcast unfinished edges of A, B and D pieces. With Black for bottom edge of boot and with matching colors, Overcast unfinished edges of C pieces.

NOTE: Cut two 16" lengths each of Denim and Lavender.

3: For each mitten, thread one 16" strand of Denim through upper right corner. Pull ends to even and tie in knot. Tie strands on each mitten together into a bow; trim ends. For motif, glue mittens together as shown in photo.

4: For each skate, with one 16" strand of Lavender, thread needle from back to front at bottom ✦ hole as indicated, pull ends to

even; working over yarn end on wrong side, insert needle back to front through each ✦ hole to top. Tie strands in knot. Tie strands on each skate together into a bow; trim ends. Glue skates together as shown.

5: For garland, untwist paper ribbon and re-twist 1" from each end and every 6"-7" in between. Glue motifs over twisted areas as shown. If desired, glue flowers and baby's breath between motifs.

GARLAND COLOR KEY:
(Amounts for one of each motif.)

#3 pearl cotton
■ Black – ½ yd.

Nylon Plus™	Needloft™ yarn
■ #02	#00 Black – 2 yds.
▨ #12	#05 Lavender – 7 yds.
▨ #06	#33 Denim – 10 yds.
▨ #40	#37 Silver – 6 yds.
□ #24	#39 Eggshell – 18 yds.
▨ #37	#53 Mermaid Green – 2½ yds.

STITCH KEY:
● French Knot

D – MITTEN
(cut 2)
19 x 22 holes

B – SNOWMAN
(cut 1)
25 x 26 holes

A – BOW (cut 1) 24 x 28 holes

Cut Out   Cut Out

C – SKATE
(cut 2)
25 x 39 holes

Cut Out

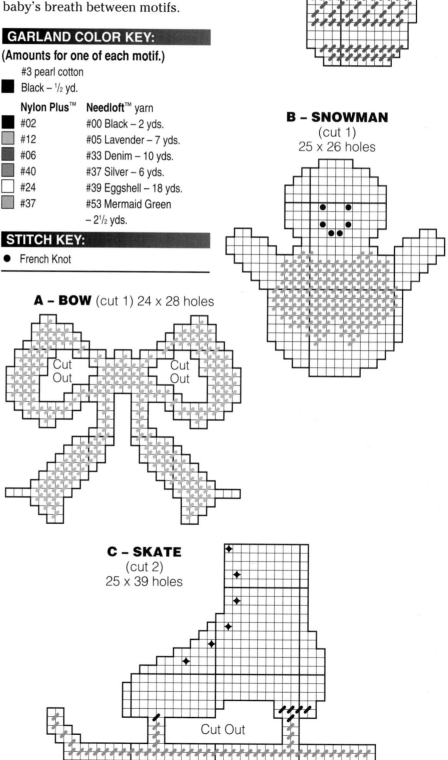

MATCH HOLDER

SIZE: 2½" square x 7⅞" tall, not including motif.

MATERIALS: One sheet of 7-count plastic canvas; Silk dried rose buds or flowers and baby's breath (optional); Craft glue or glue gun; Worsted-weight or plastic canvas yarn (for amounts see Color Key).

CUTTING INSTRUCTIONS:

A: For sides, cut four 15 x 51 holes.

B: For bottom, cut one 15 x 15 holes.

C: For bow motif, cut one according to Garland A Graph.

STITCHING INSTRUCTIONS:

1: Using colors and stitches indicated, work A-C pieces according to graphs. With Lavender, Overcast unfinished edges of C.

2: With Eggshell, Whipstitch A and B pieces together, forming holder; Overcast unfinished edges. Glue bow motif to top left corner of one side. If desired, glue flowers and baby's breath to side as shown in photo.

JAR BRIGHTENER

SIZE: Fits jar approximately 4¼" in diameter.

MATERIALS: ½ sheet of 7-count plastic canvas; Silk dried rose buds or flowers and baby's breath (optional); Craft glue or glue gun; #3 pearl cotton or six-strand embroidery floss (for amount see Color Key); Worsted-weight or plastic canvas yarn (for amounts see Color Key).

CUTTING INSTRUCTIONS:

A: For snowman motifs, cut four according to Garland B Graph on page 152.

STITCHING INSTRUCTIONS:

1: Using Mermaid Green and Continental Stitch, work A pieces according to graph. Fill in uncoded areas using Eggshell and Continental Stitch. Using pearl cotton or six strands floss and French Knot, embroider eyes and mouths as indicated on graph. With matching colors, Overcast unfinished edges.

2: Overlapping hands to fit, glue motifs together around jar. If desired, glue flowers and baby's breath to jar lid as shown in photo.✸

MATCH HOLDER COLOR KEY:

	Nylon Plus™	Needloft™ yarn
☐	#12	#05 Lavender – 7 yds.
▨	#06	#33 Denim – 40 yds.
▨	#24	#39 Eggshell – 20 yds.

B – BOTTOM
(cut 1)
15 x 15 holes

JAR BRIGHTENER COLOR KEY:

#3 pearl cotton
■ Black – ½ yd.

	Nylon Plus™	Needloft™ yarn
☐	#24	#39 Eggshell – 30 yds.
▨	#37	#53 Mermaid Green – 12 yds.

A – SIDE
(cut 4)
15 x 51 holes

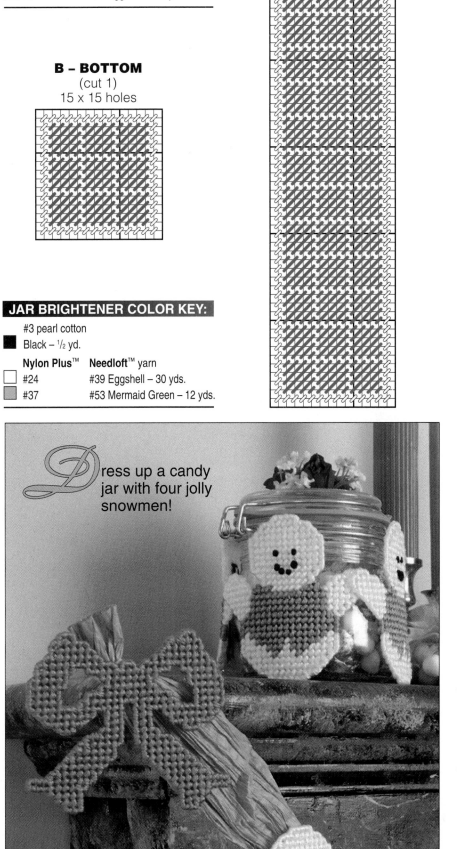

Dress up a candy jar with four jolly snowmen!

READY, SET, STITCH

BASIC INSTRUCTIONS TO GET YOU STARTED

Most plastic canvas stitchers love getting their projects organized before they even step out the door in search of supplies. A few moments of careful planning can make the creation of your project even more fun.

First of all, prepare your work area. You will need a flat surface for cutting and assembly, and you will need a place to store your materials. Good lighting is essential, and a comfortable chair will make your stitching time even more enjoyable.

Do you plan to make one project, or will you be making several of the same item? A materials list appears at the beginning of each pattern. If you plan to make several of the same item, multiply your materials accordingly. Your shopping list — complete with check-off boxes — is ready.

SUPPLIES

Yarn, canvas, needles, cutters and most other supplies needed to complete the projects in this book are available through craft and needlework stores and mail order catalogs. Other supplies are available at fabric, hardware and discount stores. For mail order information, see page 160.

NEEDLES & OTHER STITCHING TOOLS

Blunt-end tapestry needles are used for stitching plastic canvas. Choose a No. 16 needle for stitching 7-count, and a No. 18 for stitching 10-count. A small pair of embroidery scissors for snipping yarn is handy. Try using needle-nosed jewelry pliers for pulling the needle through several thicknesses of canvas and out of tight spots too small for your hand.

CANVAS

Most projects can be made using standard-size sheets of canvas. Standard-size sheets of 7-count (7 holes per inch) are always 70 x 90 holes and are about 10½" x 13½". For larger projects, 7-count canvas also comes in 12" x 18" (80 x 120 holes) and 13½" x 22½" (90 x 150 holes) sheets. Other shapes are available in 7-count, including circles, diamonds, ovals and purse forms.

10-count canvas (10 holes per inch) comes only in standard-size sheets, which vary slightly depending on brand. They are 10½" x 13½" (106 x 136 holes) or 11" x 14" (108 x 138 holes).

Newer canvas like 5-count (5 holes per inch) and 14-count (14 holes per inch) are also becoming popular with plastic canvas designers.

Some canvas is soft and pliable, while other canvas is stiffer and more rigid. To prevent canvas from cracking during or after stitching, you'll want to choose pliable canvas for projects that require shaping, like round baskets with curved handles. If your project is a box or an item that will stand alone, stiffer canvas is more suitable.

Both 7- and 10-count canvas are available in a rainbow of colors. Most designs can be stitched on colored as well as clear canvas. When a pattern does not specify color in the materials list, you can assume clear canvas was used in the photographed model. If you'd like to stitch only a portion of the design, leaving a portion unstitched, use colored canvas to coordinate with yarn colors.

Buy the same brand of canvas for each entire project. Different brands of canvas may differ slightly in the distance between each bar.

MARKING & COUNTING TOOLS

To avoid wasting canvas, careful cutting of each piece is important. For some pieces with square corners, you might be comfortable cutting the canvas without marking it beforehand. But for pieces with lots of angles and cutouts, you may want to mark your canvas before cutting.

Always count before you mark and cut. To count holes on the graphs, look for the bolder lines showing each ten holes. These ten-count lines begin in the lower left-hand corner of each graph and are on the graph to make counting easier. To count holes on the canvas, you may use your tapestry needle, a toothpick or a plastic hair roller pick. Insert the needle or pick slightly in each hole as you count.

To count a large number of holes on 7- or 10-count canvas, use the rulers on pages 156 & 157. Simply lay the edge of your canvas over the ruler, lining up the bars on the canvas with the markings on the ruler.

Most stitchers have tried a variety of marking tools and have settled on a favorite, which may be crayon, permanent marker or grease pencil. One of the best marking tools is a fine-point overhead projection marker, available at office supply stores. The ink is dark and easy to see and washes off completely with water. After cutting and before stitching, it's important to remove all marks so they won't stain yarn as you stitch or show through stitches later.

Cloth and paper toweling removes grease pencil and crayon marks, as do fabric softener sheets that have already been used in your dryer.

CUTTING TOOLS

You may find it helpful to have several tools on hand for cutting canvas. When cutting long, straight sections, scissors, craft cutters or kitchen shears are the fastest and easiest to use. For cutting out detailed areas and trimming nubs, you may like using manicure scissors or nail clippers. If you prefer laying your canvas flat when cutting, try a craft knife and cutting surface — self-healing mats designed for sewing, as well as kitchen cutting boards, work well.

YARN AND OTHER STITCHING MATERIALS

You may choose two-ply nylon plastic canvas yarn (the color numbers of two popular brands are found in Color Keys) or four-ply worsted-weight yarn for stitching on 7-count canvas. There are about 42 yards per ounce of plastic canvas yarn and 50 yards per ounce of worsted-weight yarn.

Worsted-weight yarn is widely available and comes in wool, acrylic, cotton and blends. If you decide to use worsted-weight yarn, choose 100% acrylic for best coverage. Select worsted-weight yarn by color instead of the color names or numbers found in the Color Keys. Projects stitched with worsted-weight yarn often "fuzz" after use. "Fuzz" can be removed by shaving with a fabric shaver to make your project look new again.

Plastic canvas yarn comes in about 60 colors and is a favorite of many plastic canvas designers. These yarns "wear" well both while stitching and in the finished product. When buying plastic canvas yarn, shop using the color names or numbers found in the Color Keys, or select colors of your choice.

To cover 5-count canvas, use a doubled strand of worsted-weight or plastic canvas yarn.

Choose sport-weight yarn or #3 pearl cotton for stitching on 10-count canvas. To cover 10-count canvas using six-strand embroidery floss, use twelve strands held together. Single and double plies of yarn will also cover 10-count and can be used for embroidery or accent stitching worked over needlepoint stitches — simply separate worsted-weight yarn into two-ply or plastic canvas yarn into one-ply. Nylon plastic canvas yarn does not perform as well as knitting worsted when separated and can be frustrating to use, but it is possible. Just use short lengths, separate into single plies and twist each ply slightly.

Embroidery floss or #5 pearl cotton can also be used for embroidery, and each covers 14-count canvas well.

Metallic cord is a tightly-woven cord that comes in dozens of glittering colors. Some are solid-color metallics, including gold and silver, and some have colors interwoven with gold or silver threads. Though the sparkly look of metallics will add much appeal to your project, you may substitute contrasting colors of yarn.

Natural and synthetic raffia straw will cover 7-count canvas if flattened before stitching. Use short lengths to prevent splitting, and glue ends to prevent unraveling.

FOR MORE INFORMATION

Sometimes even the most experienced needlecrafters can find themselves having trouble following instructions. If you have difficulty completing your project, write to **Plastic Canvas Editors**, *The Needlecraft Shop*, 23 Old Pecan Road, Big Sandy, Texas 75755.

CUTTING CANVAS

Follow all Cutting Instructions, Notes and labels above graphs to cut canvas. Each piece is labeled with a letter of the alphabet. Square-sided pieces are cut according to hole count, and some may not have a graph.

Unlike sewing patterns, graphs are not designed to be used as actual patterns but rather as counting, cutting and stitching guides. Therefore, graphs may not be actual size. Count the holes on the graph (see Marking & Counting Tools on page 154), mark your canvas to match, then cut. Trim off the nubs close to the bar, and trim all corners diagonally.

For large projects, as you cut each piece, it is a good idea to label it with its letter and name. Use sticky labels, or fasten scrap paper notes through the canvas with a twist tie or a quick stitch with a scrap of yarn. To stay organized, you may want to store corresponding pieces together in zip-close bags.

If you want to make several of a favorite design to give as gifts or sell at bazaars, make cutting canvas easier and faster by making a master pattern. From colored canvas, cut out one of each piece required. For duplicates, place the colored canvas on top of clear canvas and cut out. By using this method, you only have to count from the graphs once.

If you accidentally cut or tear a bar or two on your canvas, don't worry! Boo-boos can usually be repaired in one of several ways: heat the tip of a metal skewer and melt the canvas back together; glue torn bars with a tiny drop of craft glue, super glue or hot glue; or reinforce the torn section with a separate piece of canvas placed at the back of your work. When reinforcing with extra canvas, stitch through both thicknesses.

7-Count Ruler

STITCHING THE CANVAS

Stitching Instructions for each section are found after the Cutting Instructions. First, refer to the illustrations of basic stitches found on page 157 to familiarize yourself with the stitches used. Illustrations will be found near the graphs for pieces worked using special stitches. Follow the numbers on the tiny graph beside the illustration to make each stitch — bring your needle up from the back of the work on odd numbers and down through the front of the work on the even numbers.

Before beginning, read the Stitching Instructions to get an overview of what you'll be doing. You'll find that some pieces are stitched using colors and stitches indicated on graphs, and for other pieces, you will be told which color and stitch to use to cover the entire piece.

Cut yarn lengths no longer than 18" to prevent fraying. Thread needle; do not tie a knot in the end. Bring your needle up through the canvas from the back, leaving a short length of yarn on the wrong side of the canvas. As you begin to stitch, work over this short length of yarn. If you are beginning with Continental Stitches, leave a 1" length, but if you are working longer stitches, leave a longer length.

In order for graph colors to contrast well, graph colors may not match yarn colors. For instance, a light yellow may have been selected to represent the metallic cord color gold, or a light blue may represent white yarn.

When following a graph showing several colors, you may want to work all the stitches of one color at the same time. Some stitchers prefer to work with several colors at once by threading each on a separate needle and letting the yarn not being used hang on the wrong side of the work. Either way, remember that strands of yarn run across the wrong side of the work may show through the stitches from the front.

As you stitch, try to maintain an even tension on the yarn. Loose stitches will look uneven, and tight stitches will let the canvas show through. If your yarn twists as you work, you may want to let your needle and yarn hang and untwist occasionally.

When you end a section of stitching or finish a thread, weave the yarn through the back side of your last few stitches, then trim it off.

CONSTRUCTION & ASSEMBLY

After all pieces of an item needing assembly are stitched, you will find the order of assembly is listed in the Stitching Instructions and sometimes illustrated in diagrams found with the graphs. For best results, join pieces in the order written. Refer to the Stitch Key and to the directives near the graphs for precise attachments.

FINISHING TIPS

To combat glue strings when using a hot glue gun, practice a swirling motion as you work. After placing the drop of glue on your work, lift the gun slightly and swirl to break the stream of glue, as if you were making an ice cream cone. Have a cup of water handy when gluing. For those times that you'll need to touch the glue, first dip your finger into the water just enough to dampen it. This will minimize the glue sticking to your finger, and it will cool and set the glue more quickly.

To attach beads, use a bit more glue to form a cup around the bead. If too much shows after drying, use a craft knife to trim off excess glue.

Scotchguard® or other fabric protectors may be used on your finished projects. However, avoid using a permanent marker if you plan to use a fabric protector, and be sure to remove all other markings before stitching. Fabric protectors can cause markings to bleed, staining yarn.

EMBROIDERY STITCH GUIDE

FRENCH KNOT is usually used as an embroidery stitch to add detail. Can be made in one hole or over a bar. If dot on graph is in hole, come up and go down with needle in same hole. If dot is across a bar, come up in one hole and go down one hole over.

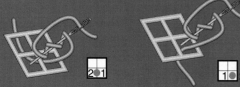

BACKSTITCH is usually used as an embroidery stitch to outline or add detail. Stitches can be any length and can go in any direction.

STRAIGHT STITCH is usually used as an embroidery stitch to add detail. Stitches can be any length and can go in any direction. Looks like Backstitch, except stitches may not touch.

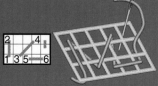

STITCH GUIDE

THE SMALL GRAPH by each illustration shows you how the stitch will look on graphs in the magazine. The numbers help you place your needle. Come up on odd numbers and go down on even numbers.

CONTINENTAL STITCH can be used to stitch designs or fill in background areas.

REVERSE CONTINENTAL STITCH

LONG STITCH can be used to stitch designs or fill in background areas. Can be stitched over two or more bars.

ALTERNATING SLANTED GOBELIN STITCH

ALTERNATING SCOTCH STITCH (OVER 3 BARS)

SCOTCH STITCH (OVER 5 BARS)

SCOTCH STITCH (OVER 4 BARS)

SLANTED GOBELIN STITCH can be used to stitch designs or fill in background areas. Can be stitched over two or more bars in vertical or horizontal rows.

WHIPSTITCH is used to join two or more pieces together.

OVERCAST STITCH is used to finish edges. Stitch two or three times in corners for complete coverage.

CROSS STITCH can be used as a needlepoint stitch on plastic canvas alone, or as an embroidery stitch, stitched over Continental Stitches with contrasting yarn or floss.

SMYRNA CROSS STITCH

RUNNING STITCH

SATIN STITCH

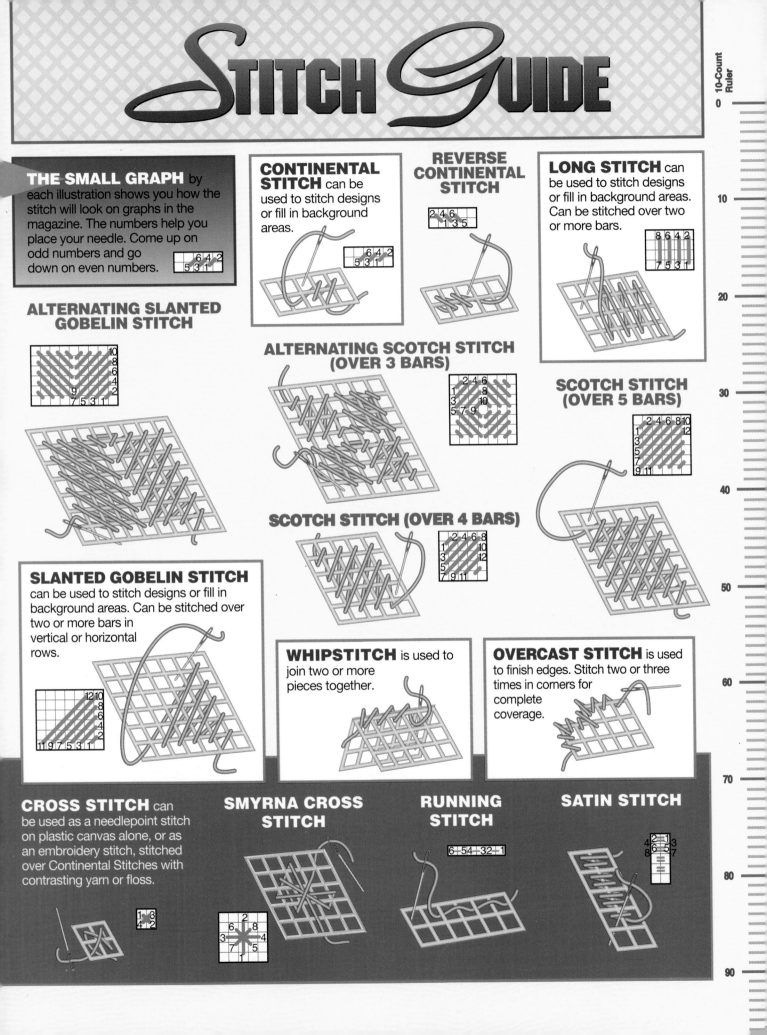

ACKNOWLEDGEMENTS

We would like to express our appreciation to the many people who helped create this book. Our special thanks go to each of the talented designers who contributed original designs.

Thanks, also, to all the talented and skilled editors, art directors, photographers and production staff whose technical expertise made the book come together.

In addition, we would like to thank the companies and individuals who provided locations for photography, models, props or other contributions.

Finally, we wish to express our gratitude to the following manufacturers for their generous contribution of materials and supplies:

AD-TECH
• Crafty Magic Melt™ Glue — Busy Babies, Victorian Fan Coasters

ALEENE'S™
• Original Designer Tacky Glue — Pastel Keepsakes

BEDFORD
• Bendable™ Decorator Ribbon — Pumpkin Goodie Jar

BEL-TREE CORP.
• E-Z Glu® Eyes — Busy Babies, Funny Friends

DARICE®
• Nylon Plus™ yarn — Li'l Critters Gift Baskets, Roses & Lace, Busy Babies, My Can-Do Book, Pumpkin Goodie Jar, Fanciful Felines, Friendly Scarecrow, Carousel Horse Doorstop, Rose Potpourri Dish, Check Mate, Hide & Seek, Country Cow Catchall, Woven Hearts
• Wedding Florals — Pastel Keepsakes
• Metallic Cord — Uncle Sam Doorstop, Check Mate, Hide & Seek, Woven Hearts
• Wooden Wheels — Tot's Tote Train
• Ultra Stiff™ canvas — Apples Galore
• Colored canvas — Friendly Scarecrow, Rose Potpourri Dish
• 10-count canvas — Romantic Greeting Cards
• 5-count canvas — Woven Hearts

DMC®
• Pearl cotton — Splish Splash, Pastel Keepsakes, Wee Wonders Nursery Set, Watermelon Baskets, Mother & Child, Happy Snowman Basket, Romantic Greeting Cards, Winter Memories
• Embroidery floss — Kitten Sachet

J.&P. COATS
• Embroidery floss — Deer Valet

KREINIK
• Metallic braid — Carousel Horse Doorstop, Romantic Greeting Cards

ONE & ONLY CREATIONS®
• Curly Hair® doll hair — Mary Had a Little Lamb

SPINRITE
• Plastic Canvas Yarn — Country Birdhouse Wreath, Wee Wonders Nursery Set

UNIEK CRAFTS
• Needloft® yarn — Splish Splash, Mary Had a Little Lamb, Let's Go Bye-Bye!, Quackers & Peanuts, Tapestry Accents, Country Welcome Sign, Uncle Sam Doorstop, Deer Valet, Tot's Tote Train, Ladybug Cozy, Welcome Door Hanging, Watermelon Baskets, Funny Friends, Apples Galore, Cherub Wreath, Holiday Memories, Mother & Child, Folk Art Angel, Joy to the World, Happy Snowman Basket, Victorian Fan Coasters, I Love Ewe, This Little Piggy, Kitten Sachet, Winter Memories
• Quick-Count® Artist Size Canvas — Tapestry Accents, Welcome Door Hanging

INDEX